CLASSIC ENGLISH DESIGN AND ANTIQUES

PERIOD STYLES AND FURNITURE

CLASSIC ENGLISH DESIGN AND ANTIQUES

PERIOD STYLES AND FURNITURE

THE HYDE PARK ANTIQUES COLLECTION

FOREWORD BY MARIO BUATTA

INTRODUCTION BY RACHEL KARR

EMILY EERDMANS

RIZZOLI
NEW YORK

FRONTISPIECE
The Little Drawing Room,
Audley End House, Saffron Waldon, Essex,
designed by Robert Adam in 1764.

Published on the occasion of the fortieth anniversary of
Hyde Park Antiques, New York.

First published in the United States in 2006 by
Rizzoli International Publications, Inc.
300 Park Avenue South
New York, NY 10010
www.rizzoliusa.com

2006 2007 2008 2009 / 10 9 8 7 6 5 4 3 2 1

ISBN 10: 0-8478-2863-8
ISBN 13: 978-0-8478-2863-0

Library of Congress Control Number: 2006927996

Designed by Abigail Sturges

Printed in China

CONTENTS

FOREWORD

Mario Buatta

Mario Buatta recreates the English country house look in a New York City townhouse with layers of porcelain, paintings, and antiques, including a spectacular George II giltwood mirror, circa 1750. Photo by Keith Meyers/ The New York Times.

My obsession with English design and antiques began early in my life, no doubt helped by spending my after-school hours with my Aunt Mary, who predated Patrick Dennis's Auntie Mame, but could have been the prototype all the same. Her house was decorated in what we now call "the English country style"—summer chintzes, winter chintzes (slipcovers), and collections of objects and furniture that whet my imagination for a real English country house, the ones filled with generations of a family's collections, exotic souvenirs from trips to the Orient, Asia, India, etc.

Aunt Mary used to take me on trips to Manhattan to shop with her decorator from W & J Sloane and that spoiled me forever. Everything was a feast for the eyes and senses. I learned about "Chickendale," "Hecklewhite," and "Chinooserie"! My quest for knowledge became inexhaustible on shopping jaunts and at the ripe old age of eleven, I purchased, on a layaway plan, a lap desk that was made of satin-wood bandings and mahogany with an Angelica Kauffman-like picture on top, hidden drawers, and a pink paper interior with fittings for pens and ink. It turned out to be an eighteenth-century piece.

As the years went on, my taste for furniture and porcelain and pottery veered very much to England. On my first trip to England as a student with the Parsons School of Design, my impressions from Aunt Mary's house finally gave way to the real thing—fabulous country houses and the exquisite Brighton Pavilion, with its extraordinary mélange of Oriental and English design.

About this time, I purchased a book on English interiors by the editors at *House and Garden*. In this book was a room that would become my favorite source of inspiration. It seemed to have been put together so lovingly with things from several centuries and countries, all beautifully arranged against walls of deep "buttah yellah," as the owner called it. The owner was the incomparable Mrs. Claude Lancaster, otherwise known as Nancy, wife to Mr. Ronald Tree and former owner of many great English country houses as well as a partner in the firm of Sibyl Colefax and John Fowler.

Eventually, I was able live out my dreams of having an apartment filled with furniture that I collected surrounded by deep yellow glazed walls and my favorite English block chintz—Floral Bouquet from Lee Jofa. As the years went by, forty-six to be exact, I "traded up" and bought better antiques, many of which were selected from the superlative collection of Hyde Park Antiques. Over the years I have found great examples of period eighteenth- and nineteenth-century English pieces for the many houses and apartments I've had the pleasure to decorate. I recall a wonderful early eighteenth-century green japanned double-dome cabinet with chinoiserie decoration that became the centerpiece of a great New York City home. Their collection is a treasure trove of exceptional objects, curated under the guidance of Bernard Karr's exquisite eye. The gallery is like a living museum, with the important difference being that you not only get to touch the objects, you have the unparalleled pleasure of being able to take them home with you.

Mario Buatta's interiors, like this pistachio green glazed sitting room, maintain a perfect balance between comfort and style, proof that living with antiques doesn't mean feeling like one is living in a museum.

A PASSION FOR COLLECTING

Rachel Karr

The sitting room in Bernard and Barbara Karr's New York apartment showcases their personal collection of Chinese export porcelain, nineteenth-century European paintings, and, of course, extraordinary English antiques.

Currently celebrating its fortieth anniversary, Hyde Park Antiques, founded in 1966 by my parents, Bernard and Barbara Karr, was the result of a life-long passion for collecting. As a boy growing up in Brooklyn, Bernard collected baseball cards, stamps, and rare coins. Then, as a young man, having developed a love for European history, he evolved a taste for objects related to that history, beginning with decorative arts and eventually furniture. While his boyhood collections could be stored in the closet of his New York City apartment, his growing assortment of furniture needed to find a larger, more permanent home.

As luck would have it, there was a vacant store near where he worked, and he thought to himself that he had enough to stock a store. If the antiques were as good as he thought, there would certainly be buyers for them. He was right, and the gallery thrived. Several years and locations later, in 1979, he acquired the spacious building that today houses the Hyde Park Collection. From that moment on, his inventory became more selective, more refined, and focused on the great periods of English cabinetry design.

Our museum-quality collection features stellar examples from the reign of William and Mary, demonstrating the period's love of walnut and marquetry; fine pieces from Queen Anne's period, when the sinuously curved cabriole leg was first introduced; and glorious works from the Georgian period, also known as the Age of Mahogany, when there was a growing interest in carved ornamentation. The collection also specializes in exemplary pieces from the Regency period

when many influences converged to create the last great examples of bench-made furniture.

A *view of a room at Hyde Park Antiques.*

My father taught me many things over the years, but perhaps the most valuable advice he has given me is to buy what you love. Buy a piece because it is a good example of its period, because you respond to it, and because you would want it in your home. He's never advocated buying fine antiques strictly for investment purposes, no doubt because he has so enjoyed living with extraordinary pieces of furniture. Given his passion, it is no surprise that over the years we have owned the same object several different times, objects he refers to as "old friends."

One of my cherished "old friends" was the first piece of furniture I fell in love with. I was about ten years old when my parents purchased a grand early George II walnut console table. It had two cherubs carved into the frieze that was festooned with foliate swags. Twelve years ago, when I had just started working at the gallery, it was offered back to us. Once again, an "old friend" stood briefly in our showroom until it found a new home.

While this volume considers the most important periods of English eighteenth- and nineteenth-century design, we hope that it will also serve as an anthology of some of the best examples of furniture available today. We invite you to our gallery to view many of the wonderful pieces that we currently have in our inventory. Here you will see how fine English antique furniture can be enjoyed in beautiful rooms created by top connoisseurs and interior decorators.

THE INTERNATIONAL COURT STYLE

WILLIAM AND MARY & QUEEN ANNE
1689–1714

Those people are gravely mistaken who imagine that all this is mere ceremony. The people over whom we rule, unable to see the bottom of things, usually judge by what they see from the outside, and most often it is by precedence and rank that they measure their respect and obedience.

—LOUIS XIV

FACING PAGE
An open doorway links to the enfilade at Petworth House, a late seventeenth-century mansion most likely designed by Daniel Marot.

For centuries, England lagged behind the Continent in innovation and luxury until political and commercial circumstances conspired to bring the latest European fashions to its insulated shores at the end of the seventeenth century. The Glorious Revolution in 1689 deposed the Roman Catholic James II and put his Protestant daughter Mary and her husband, William of Orange, Stadholder of Holland, on the throne of England and Scotland. During their reign, the craftsmanship and design of English furniture evolved to new heights of sophistication powerfully influenced by the grandiose interiors and furnishings of the French king Louis XIV's Versailles. In imitation, the palaces and great houses of England's elite were installed with ornate interiors with every surface embellished. French artisans migrated to England's shores and brought with them new techniques and fashions.

The shift of trade from within the Continent to Europe's northwest seaboard added to England's place in the world as well as to its coffers. Its strong trade links to Asia and the Americas created a thriving commercial economy, and the exponential increase in imports gave its inhabitants a taste for variety and novelty. Exotic wares from the Far East were collected zealously and displayed proudly in the houses of England's aristocracy and upper classes.

By the beginning of Queen Anne's reign in 1702, the power of the court had weakened as Parliament's ascended. A reaction against grand formality associated with absolute power set in and a deep desire for simplicity encouraged a restrained version of the Court style. The queen's intimate Sarah, Duchess of Marlborough, preferred "to have things plain and clean, from a piece of wainscot to a lady's face." One of the most important developments during this period was the increase of

furniture types which added variety to an interior's furnishings, as well as to its comfort by adapting to an owner's individual needs. In addition, luxury goods became more accessible and found their way increasingly into the homes of an emergent middle class. As the appurtenances of the good life became more widely available, more luxury goods were manufactured to suit a bourgeois sensibility. Writer Daniel Defoe observed in 1713, "Here I saw, out of a Shopkeeper's House, Velvet Hangings, Embroidered Chairs, Damask Curtains . . . in short, Furniture equal to what, formerly, suffis'd the greatest of our Nobility."

THE FRENCH INFLUENCE

Like most of Europe at the end of the seventeenth century, England's fashions followed the International Court style of Louis XIV closely. Visitors to Louis XIV's palace at Versailles, the largest and grandest secular building in Europe at the close of the seventeenth century, were stunned by its magnificent interiors and many hastened home to attempt to recreate what they had seen.

It was important to William that the appearance of his court be visually impressive, as its splendor represented the richness and power of the country itself. He brought to England from Holland highly trained designers and artisans to refurbish the royal palaces with luxurious, up-to-date furnishings. He immediately employed the architect Christopher Wren to overhaul Hampton Court as a new Versailles and replace Whitehall Palace as the main residence of the court of St. James. A visitor to Windsor Castle, the "country house" of the crown, remarked in 1698:

> . . . the cannopy was soe rich and curled up and in some places soe full it looked very glorious and newly made to give audience to the French Embassadour to shew the grandeur and magnificence of the British monarch—some of these foolerys are requisite some tymes to create admiration and regard to keep up the state of the Kingdom and nation.

The English nobility followed suit and built great houses on their country estates appointed as lavishly as their purses would allow.

The International Court style espoused by Louis XIV (r. 1661–1715) and his designers was greatly influenced by the effusive Baroque style developed during the first half of the seventeenth century in Italy to communicate the greatness of the Catholic Church. Curves, complex forms, elaborate ornament, and luxurious materials were used to incite amazement and an emotional response in the observer. The Baroque interior was designed to overwhelm a viewer with its grandeur and sumptuousness. All surfaces—walls, ceilings, floors—were elaborately treated with heavy carving, vibrant frescoes, and rich tapestries and textiles on an unprecedented scale.

Louis XIV's classical Baroque style reigned in the curves of the Roman Baroque to create a more suitably controlled and dignified version. Severe cubic forms, costly materials such as rare woods, *pietra dure*, tortoiseshell, lacquer, precious metals, and classical ornament all contributed to a solemn and imposing atmosphere. One of the most impressive rooms was the dazzling Hall of Mirrors which was extravagantly paneled with hundreds of large mirrors. This innovative and spectacular use of mirror plate was widely imitated abroad, albeit on a smaller scale. In England, it became de rigueur to include looking glasses in reception rooms, and the country's glassmakers were spurred on to attempt ever larger plates.

The vocabulary of ornament used in the rooms and furnishings at Versailles was based on the broken scroll which created the Baroque style's characteristic

Jean Berain (French, 1637–1711),
Design for a Tapestry, with
Grotesque Ornament, *c. 1680.*
Etching and engraving on white laid
paper. Cooper-Hewitt National Design
Museum, Smithsonian Institution.

A design for grotesque ornament
by the royal designer to Louis XIV
incorporates interlaced arabesques
with fanciful creatures, and was very
influential to many designers, including
Daniel Marot.

movement. However, it was applied to classical rectilinear forms with straight lines, not to the twisted and turned shapes used in Rome. This decoration was comprised of densely scrolling and interlacing arabesques or curves and is referred to as "grotesque" when incorporating foliage, animals, and other figures. Furniture inlay, ceiling decoration, textiles, and floor parquetry patterns were all enriched with this elaborate ornament.

In addition to arabesque decoration, French furniture forms, such as scrolled stretchers which joined the legs of tables and chairs together for support, pendant aprons which dipped down in imitation of swags of fabric from tables' friezes and seat rails, high backs, and Solomonic or "barley twist"-form legs later replaced by cabriole-form legs, were heartily embraced by English craftsmen. In the main, English taste was much more restrained, and the French influences included in the vocabulary of English decoration were simplified.

The use of state apartments at Versailles equally influenced the court of William and Mary. French court life revolved around elaborate ceremonial rituals, which dictated even the most quotidian of activities. Each day at Versailles began with the *lever*, when the monarch arose from the state bed attended by the crème of the French aristocracy who waited on him as he prayed, performed his daily ablutions, chose his wig, and dressed. The marquis de Saint-Maurice observed: "There is no finer sight in the world than the court at the *lever* of the King. When I attended it yesterday, there were three rooms full of people of quality, such a crowd that you would not believe how difficult it was to get into His Majesty's bedchamber." This was repeated in reverse at the *coucher*, when courtiers assembled to watch the king say his prayers, undress, and put on his nightclothes. The state bed was regarded as interchangeable with the throne and was accordingly treated as a symbol of the king's majesty. The queen had her own *lever* and *coucher* ceremonies. These court ceremonies were established to reinforce the strict hierarchy of the court and the supreme authority of the king. William and Mary and members of the nobility adopted these rituals and used the French room layout of the enfilade, a series of interconnecting reception rooms proceeding from public spaces to increasingly more private ones, which culminated in the private *appartement* of the bedchamber, dressing room, and closet. How far one penetrated the enfilade was emblematic of one's rank. The elaborate enfilade at Hampton Court consisted of the guard chamber at the top of the king's stairs, two anterooms, the Room of State where the monarch dined publicly, the withdrawing room, the bedchamber, the dressing room, and finally, the most private of all, the cabinet.

Itinerant craftsmen and engraved designs disseminated the Louis XIV style to Northern Europe. As early as 1663 it was noted that French émigré artisans "have introduced new modes and new tastes and set us all agog, and have increased among us considerable trades, witness the vast multitude of broad and narrow silk weavers, makers of looking glasses, paper, fringes and gilded leather." While traveling throughout Europe, craftsmen were exposed to the latest styles and learned various specialized skills, which, in turn, they took with them to their next place of employ.

Religious intolerance caused a mass exodus of Huguenots to flee France. In 1685, Louis XIV revoked the Edict of Nantes which had granted religious freedom to Protestants. Many Huguenots were highly skilled artisans, having been banned by the king from achieving a higher rank in France's strictly regulated hierarchical society. England extended a warm welcome to the exiled, and an order in 1681 vowed protection to the "poore distressed protestants" of France, being granted "all rights, privileges and immunities as other free Denizens do." Catholic artisans also came to England from France in the 1690s when overwhelming war debts forced the closure of the Gobelins, Louis XIV's royal workshops. As a result of the influx of these craftsmen into England, the decorative arts were enriched by their knowledge of advanced techniques and fashionable ornament.

Engraved designs were equally influential. Architects and craftsmen alike depended upon them to keep up to date on architecture, decoration, and more. Christopher Wren wrote during a 1665 visit to Paris: "I have purchased a great deal of Taille-douce [engravings] that I might give our Countrymen examples of Ornaments and Grotesks, in which the Italians themselves confess the French to excel."

The engraved designs of Daniel Marot had the greatest influence on the incorporation of French fashions in the English interior. Marot was the royal designer to William of Orange, who worked on the decoration of William III's palace of Het Loo in Holland in 1684 and on Hampton Court in the 1690s. He was born in

France into a Huguenot family of artisans and architects where he trained in the workshops of Louis XIV and became familiar with the design and decoration of the French court, until religious persecution drove him to emigrate to Holland. His designs for furniture fusing French designs with the Dutch taste were tremendously influential in developing English design, but it was his conception of the interior as a whole, with all aspects of a room relating to each other, that was Marot's greatest contribution.

THE WILLIAM AND MARY INTERIOR

You furnish her Appartement
With Morelack Tapistry, Damask Bed,
Or Velvet Richly Embroiderd:
Branches, Brasero, Cassolets,
A cofre-fort, and Cabinets,
Vases of Silver, Porcelan, store
To set, and range about the floor.
The chimney Furniture's of Plate
(For Iron's now quite out of date:)
Tea-Table, Skreens, trunks and Stand,
Large Looking-Glass richly Japan'd.

—From MARY EVELYN,
"Mundus Muliebris," 1690

An English nobleman's great house (which was really more of a palace) was viewed as "the theatre of his hospitality, the seat of self-fruition . . . the noblest of his son's inheritance, a kind of private princedom . . . an epitome of the whole world." It had

A design for a state bed by Daniel Marot, circa 1702, illustrates the importance textiles played in the decorating schemes conceived by the royal designer to William and Mary.

William's small writing closet at Hampton Court, a private space where few were granted access, is furnished with a sumptuous lacquer cabinet-on-stand and a desk in which personal documents were stowed.

FACING PAGE
The passion for needlepoint was deeply felt by Lady Mary Mordaunt who ordered this set of embroidered bed hangings and covers for six chairs and a settee for the state bedchamber at Drayton House.

a central "great chamber" or large reception room to receive important guests, which over time was commonly referred to as a saloon, an anglicized form of the French *salon*. From here, one was able to access the enfilades of the different apartments. Most great houses also featured a long gallery which served to connect different parts of the house to each other, where family portraits and other prized possessions were displayed. The pursuit of collecting gained currency with the new stimulus of imported wares that were purely decorative and many collections were proudly put on view in the gallery.

The French concept of *appartements* became fashionable amongst the nobility in England, and their houses included an apartment of state, which was used by the king and very important guests as well as additional family apartments. Following the French precedent, the state bedchamber was the most important room in the house and the climax of the enfilade. Its bed, the ultimate status symbol, was designed accordingly for maximum pageantry with the lavish and expensive textiles, less for comfort as it was seldom used. Daniel Marot's designs for the state beds of William and Mary are so dependent on upholstery that no wood at all is visible, disguised by fabric glued to the headboard and testers. The state beds were of tester form with four bed posts hung with a canopy and deep valance intricately trimmed with tassels and fringe. Curtains, suspended from the tester, were pulled close to keep in heat and provided another opportunity to use expensive material. England's cool and damp climate ensured that all but the most humble of beds were hung with fabric for warmth, privacy, and to keep out dust. Bathing was also done in one's cham-

A rare set of en suite tapestry wall hangings and seat furniture coverings dating to the seventeenth century survive at Penshurst Place.

ber with heated water brought by a servant and placed in an ewer, as bathrooms were extremely rare.

Adjoining the bedchamber was the closet or dressing room where clothing was kept. In grand apartments, the bedroom was adjoined by both a dressing room—which was where the morning levees took place and was accordingly well-appointed with a dressing table, looking glass, candlesticks, brush and comb, and other accoutrements—and a closet, often called by its French name *cabinet*. This small, intimate room might be furnished with a bureau for writing and cabinets for storing books, personal documents, and other prized possessions. This was the most personal of all rooms and was often decorated to reflect its owner's individual tastes. To gain access to the king's cabinet was a sign of great rank and privilege.

The pomp and ceremony of court life demanded appropriately lavish and stately surroundings. Every surface of the reception rooms was enriched with ornament. Walls were paneled with wood, "for so damp a country as England is, nothing could be better contrived than wainscot [oak], to keep off the ill impression of damp walls," and often painted and articulated with a cornice and chair-rail moldings. Wall hangings included heavy tapestries from Flanders illustrating classical and historical themes, and silks and damasks that could be cut to size and applied to the wall. Less grand houses sometimes had painted cloth hangings. Heavy moldings were fashionably carved, as at Windsor Castle by the master carver Grinling Gibbons, "in fruitages herbages gems beasts fowles."

Ceilings were painted with allegorical scenes or with plasterwork molded into geometric compartments enriched with fruit and foliage. Fireplaces were larger, and supported elaborate overmantels carved with armorial or allegorical subjects. Floors were made of wood or stone and arranged in geometric patterns laid upon with carpets from Turkey and Persia adding an infusion of color.

Textiles were rich, and the best upholstered furniture was covered in silk velvets and damasks from Genoa or Lyons in green or crimson, the most expensive and grandest of colors. Cotton fabric painted and printed with vividly hued decoration from India, the forebear of chintz, was extremely popular for more private and informal rooms. Needlepoint was another fashionable covering for seat furniture. Until the mid-eighteenth century, it was popular for ladies to create needlepoint panels explicitly for upholstery. Queen Mary set the example and was "oftener seen with a skein of thread about her neck than attending to affairs of state." A Bishop at court remarked that she was so addicted to needlework that she exhibited ". . . sometime with so constant a diligence as if she had to earn her bread by it. It was a new thing, and looked a sight to see, to see a Queen work so many hours a day." Executed in wool on canvas, it was also more durable and accessible than the prohibitively expensive velvets imported from Italy.

Curtains were still a luxury, and most frequently consisted of one panel pulled across the window and secured to one side. Divided curtains were used in more wealthy households, and, in rooms of state, the pull-up curtain was devised so as to keep the window hangings away from the flame of candles perched precariously nearby on tall candlestands. The complete interior schemes of Marot relied heavily

A Chinese Coromandel lacquer cabinet sits on an extravagantly carved European giltwood stand in the library at the now-dismantled Hackwood Park.

Daniel Marot (French, active The Netherlands, c. 1663–1752) Design for a Chimney Wall with Lacquered Panels and Porcelain, *from* Nouvelles Cheminées faites en plusiers endroits de la Hollande et autres provinces, *c. 1700. Etching and engraving on cream laid paper. Cooper-Hewitt National Design Museum, Smithsonian Institution.*

Daniel Marot devised an ingenious way of displaying Queen Mary's vast collection of Chinese porcelain, including brackets arranged vertically around the mantelpiece, as seen on this design for a chimney wall.

auec preuilege des Etatz geheraux des prouince Vnie

inuenté et graué par D.Marot

on upholstery and the use of wall hangings, portieres, curtains, chairs, and settees en suite. The use of the enfilade also led to uniform decoration for the connecting rooms, as it created a more pleasing vista through the doorways.

The Call of the Orient

The China trade brought all manner of exotic imports to England's shore and created a mania for chinoiserie. Holland and England's advantageous position on Europe's northwestern seaboard guaranteed these two nations an edge in the triangle trade with Asia and the Americas. The Dutch were among the first to trade with the Far East in the early seventeenth century, and the Oriental wares they imported were received enthusiastically.

England's East India Company had exclusive rights to import goods from China, and from 1663 onward it was given the right to trade with gold bullion, instead of being limited to trading with goods they exported to the East. The gold bullion enabled them to buy large quantities of lacquerware and other Oriental wares. As the company did not have permission to trade directly with Japan whose

lacquer was reputedly superior and imitated by the Chinese, Japanese products were purchased from the Dutch in small quantities at the trading post of Batavia (now Indonesia). The fashion for decorating rooms with lacquerware and porcelains originated in Holland, where they were available in quantity, and was brought to England by the court of William and Mary.

Oriental and delft ceramics were lavishly sprinkled throughout interiors, resting on wall brackets, tops of cabinets, and mantelpieces. Queen Mary had 154 pieces of porcelain in her bedchamber alone at Kensington Palace. Author Daniel Defoe wrote in *A Tour Thro' the Whole Island of Great Britain*:

> The Queen [Mary] brought in the Custom or Humour, as I may call it, of furnishing Houses with China-ware, which increased to a strange degree afterwards, piling their China upon tops of Cabinets, Scrutores, and every Chymney-Piece, to the tops of the Ceilings, and even set-ting up Shelves for their China-ware, where they wanted such places, till it became a grievance in the Expense of it, and even Injurious to their Families and Estates.

Green japanning, as seen here on a side table, circa 1715, was less common than black or red.

FACING PAGE
This important black-and-gilt japanned cabinet-on-chest, circa 1715, is surmounted by three rare ancient Chinese figures carved out of camphor wood.

Designs of porcelain supported on brackets by Pierre Le Pautre and Jean Lassurance date to the 1670s, but it was Marot who created the mania for pots piled on top of each other as shown in his design for the Queen's dressing room (see pg. 21).

The first lacquerware exported to Europe had been manufactured for the domestic market. Goods were produced in Tonkin (now Vietnam), Canton, and Amoy and sent to the East India Company's warehouses in India to be shipped back to England. Because merchant boats sailed from India, many imports were described as "Indian" indiscriminately. Among the first items of furniture to be imported was the two-door cabinet that opened to a fully fitted interior incorporating various sized drawers. In China and Japan, these cabinets sat on the floor, but in Europe, elaborate gilt stands were carved to raise them. This extremely rectilinear shape was very influential to European design, as seen in the boxiness of English cabinets and scriptors, an early form of writing cabinet raised on legs. Screens were mounted on

23

An array of exotic elements, including a japanned kneehole dresser with chinoiserie decoration, intermingle in this dramatic room by Debra Blair and Associates.

walls or cut up and applied to furniture. Trays, hand screens, stands, and small tables were all lacquer items imported to Europe. As one contemporary account states:

> As ill Weeds grow apace, so these manufactured Goods from India met with such a kind reception, that from the greatest Gallants to the meanest Cook-Maids. Nothing was thought so fit to adorn their persons as the fabric of India; nor for the ornament of Chambers like India-Skreens, Cabinets, Beds and Hangins; nor for Closets, like China and Lacquered Ware . . .

East Asian lacquer is made from a clear resin taken from the sap of the indigenous lacquer tree. As high-quality lacquerware may require up to 100 coats, with each coat drying and hardening before the next layer, its manufacture is extremely time-consuming and expensive. From its earliest manufacture in the fourth century BC, charcoal and cinnabar were mixed in to tint the lac black or red. Most often, decoration is painted on the surface, but what the English referred to as Coromandel lacquer, or Bantamwork, has its decoration carved in low relief on a gesso ground, which is then lacquered. (Bantam was the Dutch colonial post near present-day Jakarta, and Coromandel was the European name for the southeast coast of India.)

As demand increased, European designs for furniture were sent to the East where they could be reproduced in lacquer. It didn't take long before Europeans tried to replicate this material, and as they were ignorant of the lacquer tree, they used a version of lac that was taken from excretions of an Indian insect. It was collected from tree branches and sold variously as stick-lac, with the lac still on the stick; seed-lac, which was refined and in bead-form; and shell-lac, which was in the form of flakes. It was the shell-lac form was used for the imitation lacquer in combination with resins and gums.

Unlike Oriental lacquer, any color was possible with imitation lacquer because the pigments did not need to be soluble in the lacquer, but were applied directly on the object before the shellac mixture was applied. Blue, green, and white were popular as well as the traditional black and red. The raised chinoiserie decoration was made with paste of whiting (powdered chalk bound by water or oil) and bole mixed in a resin to make a paste. This mixture was applied in layers to build up the shape of a "Rock, Tree, Flower, or House . . . until tis raised as high as you think convenient . . . " The detail was then incised and finished with colored varnish, powdered metals, and penwork.

This technique was called japanning. There are references to it as early as the 1690s, but by 1700 it was commonly known. It began as a specialized technique practiced by professionals, and its advantages included a much lower cost than the Oriental lacquer and its ability to be applied to any object. Soon it became an acceptable pursuit for amateurs and young ladies. A father wrote to his daughter:

> I find you have a desire to learn Jappan, as you call it, and I approve of it; and so I shall of anything that is Good and Virtuous, therefore learn in God's name all the Good Things, & I will willingly be at the Charge so farr as I am able—tho' They come from Japan & from never so farr & Looke of an Indian Hue & Odour, for I admire all accomplishments that will render you considerable & Lovely in the sight of God and man; & therefore I hope you will perform y^R part according to y^R & employ y^R time well, & so I pray God blesse you.

John Stalker and William Parker published their *Treatise of Japanning and Varnishing* (1688), which included directions on creating the mixture and its application as well as plates of chinoiserie drawings that could be cut up and used:

> Suppose then you have a large piece of work, as a Table, or Cabinet; take one of the Prints which chiefly complies with your humour, insert others also which may be most agreeable, yet give variety too: borrow a part from one, a figure from another, birds flying or standing from a third this you may practise until your cabinet be sufficiently charged: if after all this any thing be wanting, your judgment must order, beautifie, and correct. But observe this always, that if you would exactly imitate and copie out the Japan, avoid filling and thronging your black with draught and figure, for they, as you may remark, if ever you happen to view any of the true Indian work never croud up their ground with many Figures, Houses, or Trees, but allow at a great space to little work.

Japanning reached the zenith of its popularity in the first quarter of the seventeenth century. It came back into fashion during the Regency period at the end of the eighteenth century when it was used to create the dramatic black-and-white penwork furniture. Lacquer furniture remained fashionable throughout the eighteenth century and into the nineteenth, when the Prince of Wales commissioned whimsical chinoiserie-themed rooms.

The pendulum clock was invented in 1656 in the Netherlands by Christian Huygens. It was quickly embraced by England, which, by the end of the seventeenth century, was the leading maker and exporter of longcase clocks.

Furniture

Furniture made for the William and Mary court reached an unparalleled level of elaborate construction and decoration. Gilding, inlaying, and japanning were added to the workshop's repertoire and contributed to the period's ornate interiors. The furnishings of reception rooms were primarily ceremonial, and function and practicality were secondary, if attended to at all. The purely ornamental triad used often by Marot consisted of a side table, candlestands, and mirror executed in lavish materials en suite, and was essential to achieving an appropriately grand reception room.

During Queen Anne's time, a shift in taste and a new audience of middle-class consumers resulted in furniture designed for utility and comfort. There was a move away from intricately inlaid and turned furniture decoration, and a plainer aesthetic relying on beauty of materials and simple lines was preferred now.

England didn't have the equivalent of France's royal workshops which, under the patronage of Louis XIV, were given the resources and mission to bring the applied arts to unequalled heights of sophistication. However, the craftsmen that were employed equally by the English crown and nobility were mostly foreign and had first-hand knowledge of the latest techniques and fashions from the Continent.

One of the most important additions to interiors during the seventeenth century was the looking glass, and this costly and rare innovation slowly began to populate the homes of the upper and middle classes alike. Mirrors were incorporated into the architectural fittings of rooms and were placed most frequently above the mantelpiece and on the piers between windows. Its reflection extended the room's embellishment and illumination.

The Venetian glass workshops in Murano dominated its production, but over time, the secrets of glassmaking spread throughout Europe. In 1664 there were enough English glassmakers to incorporate the Worshipful Company of Glass-Sellers and Looking Glass Makers who controlled glass production within a seven-mile radius of London.

English glass was manufactured with the "broad" process: a large tubular-shaped bubble was blown and folded outward. Size was limited by the lung capacity of the blower, and very large mirrors required several plates. The raw glass plate was ground and polished by a looking-glass maker, then finished by foiling the back to supply the reflective surface. Tin and mercury foil were used and affected a softer, slightly gray-hued reflection, in contrast to the brightness of silvering which was used predominately from 1840 onward. In contrast, the French-cast plates, a new method invented by the demands for large plates at Versailles, were made by pouring molten glass into molds, enabling plates to be much larger than those blown. The English didn't have domestic cast plates until the second half of the eighteenth century.

As production of domestic looking glasses increased, so did their accessibility. By the end of the seventeenth century, it became possible for even the middle class

ABOVE
Each pier in this room at Windsor Castle is dressed with the triad, the ultimate in ceremonial furnishings; it was comprised of a mirror, side table, and pair of candlestands.

FACING PAGE
The double-dome shape on bureau bookcases, as seen here in this romantic tented room by Dennis Rolland, evolved from the broken-arch shape made fashionable by Daniel Marot at the end of the seventeenth century. Interiors were dim and reliant on candlelight; here, candlestands slide out to support the much-needed illumination, enhanced by their reflection in the mirrored doors.

to purchase them. The plates were most often enclosed in a cushion or convex molded frame, and the more formal examples were surmounted by a detachable arched cresting that could be pierced and inlaid. From 1700 the broken arch, a derivation of the Baroque broken scroll, was prevalent in furniture forms. Marot incorporated it into many of his design schemes, and it was found in pier glasses, mirror-front doors on cabinets and bureau bookcases, and clock cases.

The largest mirrors were called pier glasses, because they were hung on the piers between windows. The arched cresting of the smaller looking glasses became mirrored, and, by 1710, these two plates were enclosed by the same outer frame. The most grand pier glasses were further enriched by carved and gilt crestings and border plates. Beveling and engraving were also extra refinements. Mirrors continued to be treated as an intrinsic part of interiors throughout the eighteenth century, and large plates remained important status symbols. Side tables were generally placed underneath pier glass. The tables at the close of the seventeenth century were raised on turned legs, and joined by cross-stretchers centered by a finial or flat space that most likely was intended to support a piece of porcelain.

As mirrors were first valued as jewelry in their earliest incarnation, the cabinet, first appearing as a table cabinet in the early seventeenth century, was equally treas-

This very early walnut and floral marquetry cushion mirror, circa 1685, retains its original detachable arched cresting. It is a particularly large example for this period, when the secrets of glassmaking were only beginning to be well-known.

ured, and given a prominent place in reception rooms. As the first portable piece of furniture for the very wealthy, it became a showpiece and emblem of status. The skill of dovetailing and making joints to construct a cabinet piece at its inception was uncommon, which enhanced its rarity and desirability. Once knowledge of cabinet-making became more widespread, its availability extended from the nobility to the wealthy and even the middle class. It is not a coincidence that the meaning of "cabinet-maker," at one point, the most coveted specialization, has developed to include the making of all types of furniture.

The cabinet was displayed in reception rooms, and was as elaborate and costly as its owner could afford. The rarity and expense of materials used for a piece were an indication to visitors of one's social status and were deliberately chosen. The earliest stands for cabinets followed side table designs closely, but increasingly they developed their own effusive style worthy of the luxurious cabinet they supported. The writing function of the cabinet gradually dictated its shape, and during Queen Anne's rule when function was valued over ostentation, it became the dominant form. The bureau cabinet or bookcase, most commonly referred to at the time as a "desk and bookcase on drawers," combined storage and function and its practicality

The mercury foil on the back of mirror plates is very susceptible to moisture which penetrates the foil and produces circular grey markings on the mirror front over time. The front of mirrors plates were beveled by hand, and the edges are wonderfully imprecise, compared to the crispness of modern machine-cutting.

ABOVE

The bold scroll-form legs on this seaweed marquetry table, circa 1690, which was once in the Untermeyer Collection at the Metropolitan Museum of Art, was fashionable at the close of the seventeenth century. A prized piece of porcelain was often placed in the center of stretchers.

RIGHT

A masterpiece of inlay and veneering, this seaweed marquetry and olivewood oyster-veneered cabinet, circa 1690, was an emblem of its owner's status.

FACING PAGE

As one of the most prestigious items of furniture at the time, this walnut bureau bookcase, circa 1710, has elaborate secret compartments which were used to store its owner's most valuable and prized possessions. Like all of the earliest "desks and bookcases on drawers," this example is made in three sections.

ensured that it was a staple for well-heeled households throughout the next century. The earliest examples are made of three parts: the cabinet, the slant-fronted writing compartment, and the chest of drawers. Over time, the chest and writing compartment were made as one piece.

Seat furniture was lined up against the walls of a room and included settees, armchairs, side chairs, and stools. It was necessary to be mindful of one's rank at all times as it dictated who sat on what. A person of high status or a guest of honor was offered an armchair, while his attendants sat on side chairs or stools. Chairs of this period have straight, tall upholstered backs, which are sometimes arched with elaborate pierced foliate decoration and caned. The tall back was a necessary support for women who were laced tightly into their dresses and supported heavy headdresses. Advances in padding and covering seat furniture at the turn of the century added tremendously to comfort. Legs were carefully turned and joined by cross-stretchers often centered by a finial in the French manner. Armrests were also turned.

At the beginning of the eighteenth century, the introduction of the cabriole leg changed the form of the English chair for the next sixty years, and resulted in what is today referred to as the Queen Anne style. The French *pied de biche*, or deer's foot terminating in a hoof or scroll, was the source of this new S-shaped leg which curved gracefully outward at the top forming a knee and inward before the foot gradually developed into the club or pad shape. The knee provided an ideal surface for some embellishment to relieve this simple chair from starkness. The complex marquetry inlay and turning of the William and Mary period was too busy for the new sober taste, and simple carved decoration such as escallop shells and acanthus foliage became customary. Seats were dropped into the chair's frame, or, for more elegant examples, upholstered over the seat rail. The curving leg was balanced by a back conformingly shaped to the human body and much shorter than the chairs of

Rideau gallonnée

Tabourets Tournée

Diferents. Rideau. de Croissée

Marot in. et fecit avec Previllige des Etats generaux et d'hollande et West. frisl.

Even after fashions had moved on, the Queen Anne style was still made for clients decades later, as on this set of chairs in the dining room at Hackwood Park, which are dated to circa 1750 by their claw-and-ball feet.

Pictorial scenes taken from printed sources were usually centered on the back of a chair in petit-point, as on this wing chair, circa 1710, observing the convention that one does not sit on people.

A walnut side table, circa 1715, reflects the preference for simplicity during the Queen Anne period.

This extremely rare bureau cabinet in the manner of Coxed and Wooster, circa 1705, has been veneered with so-called mulberry wood to simulate costly and highly fashionable tortoiseshell. Mulberry wood was usually burr maple or sycamore, stained yellow and washed over with lampblack. The staining drew out the natural figure, so a knotty and curly timber was essential. The pewter stringing would have gleamed pleasingly under candlelight.

Marot; the crest rail corresponded to the neck and shoulders, and the backsplat, in a curvaceous vase or urn shape, to the back. This resulted in an immense advance in comfort, and a diminished need for padded backs. Settees with double and triple chair backs made their appearance at this time and were made in suites with sets of chairs. The wing chair which became more prevalent was also designed for comfort; its upholstered seat, back, and sides protected the sitter from drafts.

As the interest in furniture that was useful and functional overshadowed the desire for magnificent showpieces at the beginning of the eighteenth century, a new variety of furniture types emerged that added tremendously to the comfort of living. The spread of the knowledge of joinery and dovetailing made chests of drawers, desks, and all manner of chairs and tables accessible to a larger segment of the population. The increase in choices meant that patrons were able to order as simple or complex a piece as desired and express their own individual taste. For a chest of drawers, options included a brushing slide, a kneehole, a fitted drawer with mirror and compartments, or, with the addition of a slanted top that opened to a writing surface, it transformed into a desk. "Bun" feet, turned and sphere-shaped, were used on the majority of case pieces of this period.

Fine Materials, Sophisticated Techniques

While furniture forms were evolving slowly and remained relatively simple, the materials and decorative touches used—such as gilt, beautifully figured woods, and intricate marquetry—enlivened the pieces spectacularly. Gilt furniture was the most grand and found only in the royal palaces and houses of the nobility. Gold was exorbitantly expensive, and its surface was delicate, preventing it from serving any practical function. Over time, mirror frames were most often treated with this technique and continue to be so. Hanging on the wall, a frame was protected from wear and tear, and the glass plate it enclosed added to the brilliance and luminosity of the gold frame.

In most upper-class households, it was walnut that dominated. During this period, an ingenious variety of ways of laying on veneers was conceived. The diarist John Evelyn wrote in his ode to wood, *Sylva*:

> . . . in the Wall-nut, you shall find, when 'tis old, that the Wood is admirably figured, and as it were marbl'd, and therefore much more esteemed by the Joyners, Cabinet-makers, &c. then the Young, which is paler of Colour, and without any notable Grain, as they call it. For the Rain distilling along the Branches, when many of them break out into clusters from the stem, sinks in, and is the Cause of these marks . . .

ABOVE
A walnut kneehole adds function to this burl walnut chest, circa 1715, making it usable as a desk and dressing table.

FACING PAGE
Sophisticated floral marquetry decoration is inlaid in an array of contrasting timbers into this walnut tallcase clock by Christopher Gould, circa 1695, in this townhouse sitting room by William Rush Jenkins.

England imported walnut from France and Virginia. Although French walnut was the most favored as its figure was thought to resemble the veinings of marble—"as that which we have from Bologne is very black of Colour, and so admirably streaked . . . "—war and limited supply caused the more straight-grained black walnut from Virginia to be much used in the eighteenth century. Because of its scarcity, walnut was applied in thin sheets of veneer onto a carcass of a less expensive wood. Oak, because of its denseness and durability, was more often used for higher quality items. It is also common to find the carcass one timber and the dust boards (i.e., the wood planks between drawers) and drawer linings of another. In addition to walnut, yew, laburnum, kingwood, chestnut, olive, holly, beach, sycamore, and fruitwood were used.

The application of veneers was carefully considered and designed to enhance the form of the piece as well as to take advantage of the figure of the wood's grain itself. The edges of most walnut chests and cabinets were banded, which in addition to being decorative, provided protection against wear. In the eighteenth century, featherbanding became prevalent, which took advantage of the wood grain to create a herringbone effect. Over time, featherbanding became more refined and narrow and can be a useful tool to dating a piece.

FACING PAGE
The vibrancy of this walnut, oyster-veneered, and floral marquetry cabinet-on-stand, circa 1695, serves as a reminder as to how colorful furniture was when first made.

BELOW
This detail of broad featherbanding on a walnut chest-on-chest indicates an early date of 1700. Over time, this technique became narrower and more refined.

A walnut chest, circa 1695, is spectacularly enlivened with vibrant floral marquetry panels.

FACING PAGE
The striking juxtaposition of light and dark inlay on this extraordinary seaweed marquetry cabinet-on-chest, circa 1695, and the sense of swirling movement created by the intricate scrollwork are quintessential Baroque features.

FAR LEFT
A pen-and-ink design for grotesque ornament by Daniel Marot, circa 1690, incorporating foliate strapwork with flowers, birds, and musicians, reveals his French training and the influence of the French designer Jean Berain.

LEFT
An arched cresting like those used on mirrors graces the bonnet of this seaweed marquetry longcase clock by William Loaden, circa 1695.

Floral marquetry was one of the signature elements of the International Court style and originated from Louis XIV's royal workshops. The first extant example was by Pierre Gole in 1661 and incorporated wonderfully naturalistic sprays of flowers and foliage. The extremely fashionable still-life paintings of abundant floral bouquets by such artists as Jean-Baptiste Monnoyer were engraved and sold in volumes, which provided inspiration to inlayers.

The French royal workshops worked from a master drawing, unlike their English contemporaries. English inlayers, instead, rearranged pieces of a pattern to create different designs. Once the pieces were laid out, the ground was marked and sawn out separately. This also enabled inlayers to enlarge or reduce the ground to adjust to the different sizing of graduated drawers. The pieces could then be shaded or dyed as desired. John Evelyn described this process:

> . . . when they would imitate the natural turning of leaves in their curious Compartments and bordures of Flower-works, they effect it by

Identical arabesque panels, as seen on this walnut chest of drawers, circa 1690, were cut from veneers at one time, unlike in floral marquetry.

dripping the pieced (first cut into shape and ready to In-lay) so far into hot Sand, as they would have the shadow and the heat of the Sand darkens it so gradually, without detriment or burning the thin Chip, as one would conceive it be natural.

Inlayers took advantage of the natural range of colors found in the varieties of wood, and also dyed them an assortment of colors to achieve an extremely vibrant jewel-box effect. Detailed instructions for dying wood and other materials such as bone and ivory, were given in contemporary trade books. For example, bone was dyed green with concoctions of nitric acid or, for another shade of green, with copper filings. Generally, softer woods, such as sycamore or boxwood, were preferred for dying as they absorbed more color.

Particularly Baroque in style, seaweed or endive marquetry was immensely popular until about 1715. It consisted of elaborate foliate scrollwork or arabesque decoration based on the acanthus leaf in contrasting light and dark timber. It was known at the time as filigree. Unlike floral marquetry, all its elements were cut at one time. The most sophisticated practitioner of this style was Gerrit Jensen (fl. 1680–1715) who has been called "the English Boulle," after André-Charles Boulle, who created elaborate marquetry pieces in this style for Louis XIV. Jensen produced fabulous pieces for the palaces of William and Mary in both wood and metal marquetry.

Of all the forms of marquetry, oyster veneering took the most advantage of the grain of the timber used. Transverse or oblique cuts were taken to form ovals which were then laid on the carcass in concentric circles and other geometric patterns, and outlined with banding or stringing. Cutting the veneer in this way was also a practical and economic use of wood. Walnut, olive, kingwood (so called because of its extremely high cost), and laburnum were often used for oyster veneering.

Every surface of this walnut chest of drawers, circa 1700, is inlaid with oyster veneers.

ᘓ ᘓ ᘓ

At the close of Queen Anne's reign, a change in political climate created a desire for a new national style that was independent from the glitter and absolutism of Versailles. The sumptuous and elaborate interiors of William and Mary, which first represented the prestige and wealth of England, were soon associated with excess and hedonism:

> How affected and licentious are the works of Bernini and Fontana. How wildly extravagant are the Designs of Borromini, who has endeavoured to debauch mankind with his odd and chimerical beauties, where the parts are without Proportion, solids without their true bearing, Heaps of Materials without strength, Excessive Ornaments without Grace, and the Whole without Symmetry.

FACING PAGE

Broad fruitwood banding contrasts dramatically with dark walnut on this chest of drawers, circa 1695, creating a contemporary graphic effect in this bedroom by William Rush Jenkins.

The arts and architecture of ancient Rome provided an example of harmony and order that was the foundation of England's own national style, and soon the ornate styles that had been the model were eschewed for the more sober and restrained precedents of antiquity.

A NEW BEGINNING

THE PALLADIAN STYLE
1715–1740

To build, to plant, whatever you intend,
To Raise the Column, or the Arch to bend,
To swell the Terra, or to sink the Grot,
In all let Nature never be forgot.
—ALEXANDER POPE

The search for a national identity and style took England on a unique departure from the rest of Europe in the second decade of the eighteenth century and back in time to the classical architecture of ancient Rome. England's flourishing economy and expansion, the ascension of a Protestant monarch, and a virulent antipathy to Catholic expressions of style provided fertile ground for the development of the Palladian style.

George I, Elector of Hanover, was fifty-ninth in line for the throne when Queen Anne died, but was chosen as her successor in 1714 because he was not of the Catholic faith. A bishop wrote at the time, "A Protestant country can never have stable times under a Popish Prince." Catholics believed in the divine right of kings, and, in England, the religion itself came to be associated with the corruption and repression symptomatic of absolute rule. Parliament, led by the anti-Catholic Whig party, had ensured that the next sovereign after Anne would be Protestant by passing an Act of Settlement, and consequently protected its own power.

The courts of William and Mary and Anne, like the rest of Europe, had followed the modes and fashions of the French court. Now, besmirched by associations with France's Roman Catholic monarchy, they were no longer acceptable to emulate and were patriotically rejected. England's new king had no interest in leading taste; George I spent little time in England and his son George II, who shortly followed him onto the throne in 1727, made little effort to bring high fashion to the court. Instead, it was the aristocracy who dictated England's new national style.

A period of spectacular growth and prosperity commenced under the rule of the House of Hanover. England successfully led the coalition to curtail the French conquest for European dominance, and emerged from the 1713 Peace of Utrecht with its

This seventeenth-century Italian capriccio of classical ruins, showcased here by interior designer Charlotte Moss, is typical of the souvenirs the English mi' lords brought back from their Grand Tours.

FACING PAGE
A drawing of an arch from the 1738 English translation of Palladio's Four Books of Architecture.

international reputation strengthened. Outside of Europe, Britain's land holdings in North America and the West Indies were expanding, and its trade with India and China flourished. England's cities and towns also thrived. Between 1700 and 1750, Manchester, Leeds, and Nottingham all doubled in population, and London was the largest city in Western Europe, which made it the nation's natural capital of industry and taste. Trade and manufacturing made many fortunes, and the wealthy consumer was now able to find native-made products equal in sophistication and quality to anything made elsewhere in Europe. These wares, accoutrements of a fashionable lifestyle, were in high demand by a burgeoning middle class of bankers, land owners, merchants, and manufacturers. These new riches also resulted in an enormous building boom throughout the country, and aristocrats, the arbiters of taste, searched for a distinct British style appropriate for these new buildings and public monuments.

The Grand Tour played an essential role in directing the taste of these aristocrats. By the beginning of the eighteenth century, the Grand Tour was the culmination of a young British nobleman's education. Over the course of a year or more, a "mi' lord," accompanied by his chaperone or "governor," observed firsthand monuments and antiquities described in the ancient Roman and Greek writings he had spent years studying.

The contemplation of these classical works of art was thought to provoke a deeper understanding of virtue. Anthony Ashley Cooper, third Earl of Shaftesbury, whose writings on the importance of morality and virtue were extremely influential, declared: "One who aspires to the character of a man of breeding and politeness is careful to form his judgment of arts and sciences upon right models of perfection." The belief that antiquity provided the "right model" and should be imitated was the first step towards modeling the new National style after that of the ancients.

Spoils from their travels, such as marble busts, velvet damasks, cameos, and paintings of classical ruins were brought back to enrich the mi'lords' great houses.

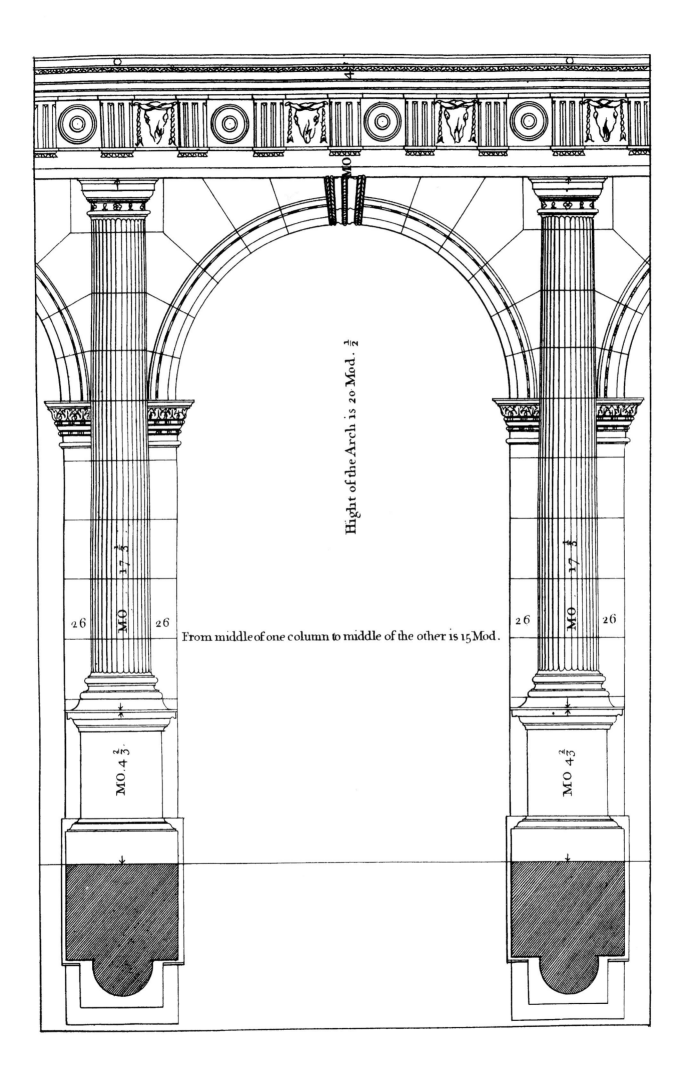

Hight of the Arch is 20 Mod. $\frac{1}{2}$

From middle of one column to middle of the other is 15 Mod.

26   MO. 17 $\frac{1}{5}$ 26

MO. 4 $\frac{2}{3}$

26   MO. 17 $\frac{1}{5}$ 26

MO 4 $\frac{2}{3}$

The insatiable acquisitiveness of the English during their travels resulted in the creation of new items for consumption; their desire for visual souvenirs of the sites they had seen prompted an enormous output of Italian topographical paintings. Canaletto, one of the most famous painters of this time, relied almost solely on an English clientele and used the English Consul, Joseph Smith, as agent. The Italian government soon imposed restrictions on the exportation of ancient artifacts, and the English made due with marble copies and plaster casts of the originals. The mid-century excavations of Pompeii and Herculaneum fueled the fascination the English held for the classical world through the century and into the next.

It was during the Grand Tour that Richard Boyle, third Earl of Burlington and fourth Earl of Cork, became, like many of his compatriots, an Italophile. In 1715 he brought back hundreds of trunks of souvenirs, and a passionate commitment to promote classical arts in his homeland which would make him the most powerful tastemaker of his time and earn him the title "Apollo of the Arts." He commissioned Giovanni Maria Bononcini and George Frideric Handel to write Italian operas, and Giovanni Battista to make classically inspired statues. A building appropriate in style to house his new treasures was his next endeavor, and he collaborated with the Scottish architect Colen Campbell to refurbish his London home, Burlington House.

It was the work and publications of Andrea Palladio, the sixteenth-century Venetian architect, which provided the inspiration for Burlington House and the new Palladian style. Palladio was a minor architect who designed numerous villas and churches in the Veneto region. He modeled his buildings after the classical Roman principles espoused in *De architectura*, the first-century-AD writings of the ancient Roman military engineer Marcus Vitruvius Pollio.

Vitruvius declared that "Architecture depends on order" because "Order gives due measure to the members of a work considered separately, and symmetrical agreement to the proportions of the whole." Order, in turn, was essential as it was based on nature, the ultimate example of perfection. The philosopher George Berkeley rhapsodized: "Oh Nature! Thou art the fountain, original and pattern of all that is good and wise . . . You wou'd like then to follow Nature, and propose her as a guide and pattern for your imitation." Five classical styles, known as orders, were outlined by Vitruvius. The Doric, Tuscan, Ionic, Corinthian, and composite orders each consisted of a column, shaft, capital, and entablature with strictly defined ornament and proportions. Throughout the eighteenth century, familiarity with the orders was essential to the education of a cultured gentleman as well as for artists and artisans.

It was Palladio's interpretation of Vitruvius's writings in *I Quattro Libri dell'Architectura*, published in 1570, that resulted in his posthumous fame. Palladio's version of *I Quattro Libri* used his own designs as illustrations, thereby establishing his application of Vitruvius's principles as *the* classical model to imitate. Venetian or arched windows, pillared porticoes, and expanses of unembellished space were Palladio trademarks.

In 1715 two publications that proselytized the virtues of classical architecture to the English were released: an English translation of *I Quattro Libri* and *Vitruvius Britannicus*. *Vitruvius Britannicus* was written by Burlington's architect Colen Campbell, and consisted of three volumes of engravings of seventeenth-century and early eighteenth-century English buildings. In the preface Campbell extolled the legacy of Palladio: "the great Palladio, who has exceeded all that were gone before him and surpassed his contemporaries, whose ingenious labours will eclipse many and rival most of the Ancients." Campbell singled out the seventeenth-century British architect Inigo Jones, and praised him as a "native" practitioner of the classical style, which helped the Palladians present this as a national style.

Exposed to Palladio's work in Venice, Jones was a pioneer of the Palladian style in England. As the principal architect for the court of James I and Charles I, Jones designed the Whitehall Banqueting House (1619–22) and the Queen's House at Greenwich (1616–35), adhering strictly to classical principles. Ironically, when the king was overthrown in 1642, Jones was tainted by his associations to the Catholic court and his career declined. Jones's work and engraved designs, which earned him the title of the English Palladio, came to provide much needed guidance for the Palladian interior.

Aristocrats all over Britain soon followed Burlington's lead and provided themselves with Palladian mansions and villas in which they could enjoy their surrounding estates. Prime Minister Robert Walpole commissioned Campbell to build the most extravagant power house of the day, Houghton Hall, in 1722, and Lord Burlington himself with his protégé and close companion, William Kent, designed Holkham Hall for Thomas Coke, first Earl of Leicester, in 1734, and the masterpiece Chiswick House in 1725, a temple to the arts designed not as a residence but as a repository for Burlington's collections. The stately home adorned with columns and pediment became a feature of the British countryside.

THE PALLADIAN INTERIOR

The gradual shift away from ceremonial court life and the emerging trend of more informal socializing created major changes in the use and layout of public spaces. People began to gather in "assemblies," "a stated and general meeting of polite per-

The famous double-cube room measuring sixty feet long and thirty feet high at Wilton House, home of the Earl of Pembroke, was created by Inigo Jones's nephew and pupil John Webb circa 1649 (most likely with Jones's involvement), and is an example of Jones's interpretation of Palladio's designs that so influenced William Kent and his contemporaries. The room is furnished with eighteenth-century furniture by Kent.

This painting by William Hogarth depicts an assembly at the opulent Wanstead House, home of the banker Sir Robert Child and the first Palladian house, designed by Colen Cambell. Guests play cards, take tea, and cluster in several groupings—a change from the formal ceremonies of court life of only a few decades earlier.

sons of both sexes, for the sake of conversation, gallantry, news, and play." Not only did a large reception room become essential, but all reception rooms were used equally. The linear processional enfilade of the Baroque period in which access to certain rooms was dictated by one's social status was outmoded, and new arrangements of rooms leading off the hall were devised to support an equality of use. The departure from the enfilade in which rooms opened up into each other also enabled each room's interior to be conceived individually featuring different colors of wall hangings and furniture upholstery.

The Palladian house was designed with the most important rooms on the *piano nobile*, or first floor (for Americans, the second floor). It was accessed by ascending the stairs in the Great Hall, which, as the point of entry and first impression, was as magnificent and imposing as possible. On the *piano nobile* were the reception rooms and the state bedchamber which in many houses, by mid-century, was all that remained of the state apartment. The insular personalities of George I and George II didn't encourage the planning of large state apartments for royal visits, and so the seldom-used state bedchamber served solely as an emblem of status and wealth.

The enormous expansion of cities at this time resulted in the building of many terraced housing developments with uniform Palladian facades for the middle class. The common plan for a space-constricted townhouse was two rooms on each floor: a double drawing room on the first floor, which also served as the main reception room, bedchambers and dressing rooms above, and the kitchen and offices or family parlor on the ground level.

The drawing room, a term truncated from "with-drawing room," was entered upon after withdrawing from the ceremonial levee, or in more modest households, from the dining room. The custom of women retiring to the drawing room after dinner and the men remaining to drink and smoke set the tone for decoration. The dining room was considered a more masculine room and treated more conservatively and sparingly with old family portraits, silver, and old-fashioned furniture. In contrast, the drawing room was fitted as up-to-date and luxuriously as possible—qualities considered more feminine.

Few English interiors were conceived with a complete classical order, but elements, such as columns and pediments, were applied to door frames, chimneypieces, and furniture alike in accordance with the English sense of status and rank.

This painting by Joseph Francis Nollekens depicts Earl Tylney and his family and friends in a grand Palladian interior at Wanstead House. Heavy pediments hang over the doorways and overmantel, and a Kent-style gesso side table is on the right. The walls are painted drab, embellished with gilt detailing.

Depending on the size and grandeur of a house, the *piano nobile* might be adorned with Corinthian columns, pilasters, moldings, and ceiling height while elements of the Doric, the least ornate order, were found in the basement. The dado and cornice were molded in size and intricacy appropriate to the importance of the room. Door frames were massive and supported boldly carved friezes and pediments.

A reception room in a great house was often painted an expensive blue, made from smalt or verdigris. The Palladian taste for undecorated expanses of space as well as the drawback of fabric's absorption of smoke, soot, and odors, contributed to the preference for painted walls rather than wall hangings. Plaster walls and ceilings were enriched with boldly carved classical ornament picked out in gold. Stuccoists and plasterers enjoyed a brisk trade and were key to creating the architectural articulation desired by Kent and his followers. A more modest house had painted wainscoted walls paneled in squares and rectangles in muted shades of green, yellow, and off-white. Ceilings were plastered and painted an off-white.

The gilt frame of the mirror, circa 1725, over the mantel adds a stunning accent to the blue-and-cream color scheme in this sitting room by Pamela Banker.

Festoon pull-up curtains with pelmets were de rigueur by now for windows. Imported damasks and silk velvets still reigned as the most desirable and costly of textiles, while the lightweight chintz from India was equally enjoyed in less important rooms and modest households for its affordability and washability. A costly and vividly hued carpet imported from Persia or Turkey lay on the deal or oak floorboards, as only the entrance-hall floor was able to support the weight of exorbitantly expensive marble arranged in geometric patterns. The overall effect of symmetry and controlled use of ornament was a stark contrast to the ornate spaces of William and Mary, in which every surface was treated with decoration. Grandeur was communicated in the Palladian room by transforming it into a classical temple.

ABOVE LEFT
Classical ornament such as scallop shells and cornucopiae are finely carved into this gilt gesso mirror, circa 1735.

ABOVE RIGHT
The triangular pediment of this white painted mirror from 1735 is derived from the architecture of ancient temples.

Furniture

While there were explicit designs for Palladian building exteriors, none existed for an interior's furnishings. It was the painter, decorator, landscape architect, and protégé of Lord Burlington, William Kent, whose solution set the style for Palladian style furnishings. Kent met Burlington in 1719 in Italy, while working as a painter, and returned with him to live at Burlington House. Burlington promoted Kent enthusiastically and sponsored Kent's publication of the *Designs of Inigo Jones*, which included more designs by Kent, Burlington, and Jones's pupil John Webb than by Jones himself. He also secured commissions for Kent to oversee the interiors of a number of great houses. Robert Walpole's son and man-about-town Horace Walpole dubbed Kent Lord Burlington's "proper priest" in the cult of Palladio, and

Sunburst inlay, checkerbanding, and classical fluted corners distinguish this chest of drawers, circa 1730.

This grand chest-on-chest, circa 1735, pays homage to the classical orders with gilt Corinthian capitals. A drawer is ingeniously fitted with pigeonholes and hinges down to work as a writing surface.

FACING PAGE
A richly hued walnut chest of drawers, circa 1725, warms up a pale green bedroom.

remarked that his "fame and popularity in his own age were so great, that he was employed to give designs for all things, even for those which he could know nothing about—such as ladies' birthday dresses, which he decorated with the five orders of architecture."

Kent's decoration of interiors and designs for furniture relied heavily on Jones as well as on Italian examples Kent had observed while living abroad. His particular challenge was to adapt these effusive Baroque models to fit into the restrained Palladian interior. One way he addressed this was to furnish a room sparingly but with monumentally scaled and boldly carved furniture so that tables, chairs, and mirrors were experienced as sculpture. He liberally applied a repertoire of motifs, including classical masks, escallop shells, Vitruvian scrollwork, fish scales, and the acanthus leaf to walls, ceilings, and furnishings.

William Kent's furniture was massive and he typically furnished "A hall or saloon, large enough to receive a company of sixty or a hundred persons . . . with six or eight chairs, and a couple of tables" like the extraordinary one illustrated here (from a pair), circa 1730.

TOP

The legs on this 1739 design for a side table by William Jones cleverly fuses the Kentian S-scroll with the cabriole leg ending in paw feet.

ABOVE

With the addition of a plinth base, these console tables are almost identical to William Jones's design.

Classically fluted pilasters and rich walnut enrich an imposing bureau bookcase in this study by William Rush Jenkins.

Considering the increasing scarcity of walnut, this handsome chest-on-stand made of the expensive wood, circa 1720, featuring unusual inlay, would have reflected well on its owner's wealth and taste.

Only the most wealthy and fashion-forward households contained Kentian furniture—it was impractical and unusable for daily life. For the merely genteel, rooms were of a much smaller scale and consequently weren't a suitable showcase for this colossally sized furniture. There were also fewer rooms, so it was necessary for each room to serve more functions and contain a wider range of furniture types.

In addition to the application of classicism to furniture, another major change in the appearance of furniture was its execution in mahogany instead of walnut. The dark hardwood was imported by the Dutch and the Spanish from the West Indies, and after a tariff on its importation was lifted in 1721, it soon became the dominant timber for furniture.

Among mahogany's virtues was its strength, which made it easier than walnut to carve and shape into curvier forms such as the cabriole leg. Larger planks were available, and its dense grain ensured that it wasn't prone to worm damage or warping as easily as the softer walnut. Marquetry inlay had almost entirely vanished. Its intricate and swirling appearance did not complement the symmetrical and restrained Palladian interior. The resemblance of highly polished mahogany with carved decoration to sculpted marble would have been particularly pleasing to the eyes of Lord Burlington and his followers. Kent's preferred furniture materials were gesso—painted and gilt—and mahogany, which he used extravagantly. The cost of a massive mahogany doorway of the saloon at Houghton Hall alone cost £1000.

Gilt gessowork was introduced to England by the Huguenot émigré gilders Jean, Thomas, and René Pelletier who brought knowledge of this technique from France during the reign of William and Mary. The soft wood carcass of an object was coated with gesso, a soft gypsum paste, that was carved or incised in low relief. A layer of bole, a type of clay, then gold leaf was applied and burnished. The uncarved areas were often punched which, like the faceting of a gemstone, reflected more light and made the piece literally more dazzling. Gesso furniture painted white and gray was also appreciated for its likeness to Italian marble statuary.

Walnut pieces were still available to and in demand by the very wealthy. The increasing scarcity of walnut due to constant deforesting and harsh winters made it very costly indeed. Chests, cabinets, bureau bookcases, and writing desks were made in quantity. Chests-on-chests or stands were updated with architectural elements, such as fluted pilasters, and sometimes inlaid with a sunburst, a motif originating in the Netherlands and the only remaining use of marquetry decoration. They were now made with bracket-shaped feet, instead of turned bun feet.

In all households, both aristocratic and middle class, the chimneypiece was the focal point of a room and was modeled after late sixteenth-century and early seventeenth-century Baroque examples. Kent applied Jones's designs of pedimented chimneypieces and painted ceiling decoration directly at Sir Thomas Coke's Holkham Hall. Contemporary drawing books, such as Kent's, devoted several pages to various

This rare and very large giltwood overmantel mirror, circa 1725, encloses an exquisite oil painting of a rural landscape scene. The intricate cartouche (detail) was most likely an armorial of its owner.

designs of appropriate chimneypieces. Over the mantel was placed an important painting or a mirror enclosed in a heavy frame worked with the same vocabulary of the room's architectural ornament. Mirrors were also placed over side tables in the piers between windows. The matching candlestands of the Baroque triad were no longer fashionable; instead they were placed in the corners of the room.

For the first time, mirrors were designed by architects and became an intrinsic part of a room's decorative scheme, causing larger numbers than ever before to be produced. The frame was often surmounted by an architectural pediment: the broken arch and swan's neck forms were both popular, often enclosing a shell, cartouche, armorial, or other ornament. They were most often entirely gilt, or made of mahogany or walnut with some gilt decoration. More than any other items of furniture, mirrors (and to a lesser extent side tables) copied Kent's heavy and richly carved designs most closely. Their placement in the main reception rooms, where it was important to be as up-to-date as possible, no doubt serves as part of the explanation.

Side tables were treated enthusiastically with boldly scrolling legs, betraying Jones's Baroque influence, and deeply incised classical ornament. Bird or animal supports such as eagles and dolphins were also popular. Supporting marble, mosaic, or scagliola (imitation marble) tops, they were executed in gilt or painted gesso. The possession and connoisseurship of various types of marble and stone was tremendously appealing to the virtuosi and architects of the period, and Italy was scoured for rare specimens. A more restrained variety of the side table that resisted Kent's influence was prolific; a marble or wood top was supported on cabriole legs and carefully enriched with classical motifs.

Wall brackets and pedestals were newly introduced into the English interior and found their way into Palladian halls, dining rooms, and libraries, where they showcased busts, urns, and bronzes. They were architectural in design and conceived as part of a room's fittings.

A walnut and parcel gilt overmantel mirror, circa 1730, retains its original beautifully chased brass candlearms.

FACING PAGE
The dining room at St. Giles, home of the Earl of Shaftesbury whose writings on virtue held great sway over Lord Burlington and his contemporaries, is illuminated with an oval pier mirror seamlessly integrated into gilt plasterwork.

This spectacular walnut and parcel gilt mirror, circa 1735, is carved with fruit swags and foliate C-scrolls that hint at the nascent Rococo style.

FACING PAGE
An Irish walnut "tabernacle" mirror by John and Francis Booker reflects the antiques-laden hall of the home of Bernard and Barbara Karr.

The use of occasional furniture, which could be moved around a room, and sets of upholstered seat furniture, added to the comfort and informality of interiors. The fashion of ordering seat furniture en suite trickled down to more modest households. When not in use, it was arranged around the wall, and pulled into the center or even brought into another room as needed. Seats upholstered in leather, damask, or needlepoint replaced less comfortable caned or rushed ones. Upholstered backs were preferred for reception rooms. Chairs used in more informal rooms and provincial households had the traditional form of the solid baluster or urn-shaped backsplat. Legs were of a more pronounced cabriole shape, enabled by the new use of mahogany, and the stretchers disappeared. The increase of carved decoration led the pad or club foot, a plain, rounded, flat termination, to gradually be supplanted by a delineated scroll-, paw-, or claw-and-ball foot. The claw-and-ball form evolved

This early mahogany example of a library desk, circa 1735, now in the anteroom at Spencer House, is related to the celebrated "owl" tables made by the carver John Boson for Lord Burlington at Chiswick House.

from the English fascination with the Chinese, and represented a dragon's foot clutching the pearl of wisdom. Arms on chairs commonly terminated in lion masks and eagle head decoration. Kent's chairs departed completely from this form, and were inspired by highly decorative and almost unusable Venetian Baroque examples. They were supported on broken S-scrolls, curule-form legs, and tapering legs, similar to his side tables.

Small tables ingeniously designed for multiple purposes made their entry into drawing rooms and parlors. Playing cards was an intensely popular pastime, and tables, often found in pairs, were designed to accommodate games. Horace Walpole wrote, "Whist has spread an universal opium over the whole nation; it makes courtiers and patriots sit down to the same pack of cards." Faro (or pharaoh), piquette, and ombre were fashionable games, and Walpole recorded two tables set up

FACING PAGE
A magnificent mahogany side table supports a marble slab top in Bernard and Barbara Karr's formal dining room.

RIGHT
The pinched paw feet and deep apron carved in low relief similar to gilt gessowork are telltale characteristics of this mahogany side table's Irish origins, circa 1735.

Custom blue-gray and white upholstery on a library armchair, circa 1740, pays homage to Pauline de Rothschild's famous London apartment in this sumptuous room by Alex Papachristidis.

Beautifully carved mahogany legs on this side chair, circa 1740, gleam like marble statuary.

As seat furniture was generally placed against the wall when not in use, back legs were usually left plain. When all four legs of a library armchair were fully finished, as on this mahogany example, circa 1745, it was an extra refinement which cost the client and elevated the chair above the standard.

A corner chair was designed expressly to fit in the corner of a room.

A mahogany armchair, circa 1725, is crisply carved with scallop shells and the new claw-and-ball foot.

This rare library armchair, circa 1735, upholstered in petit- and gros-point needlework, is made of the scarce and costly walnut, not mahogany, which was customary.

This handsome walnut double-chair-back settee, circa 1740, is vigorously carved with lion's head armrest terminals, lion mask carved knees, and hairy paw feet.

The X-frame supports on this unusual pair of walnut armchairs, circa 1750, once at Bryanston House, Dorset, were derived from ancient throne chairs and were used more frequently during the Regency period decades later.

A 1744 design for an armchair by William Kent is influenced by Venetian Baroque examples and bears little resemblance to mainstream English chair design.

BELOW
A very rare gilt gesso armchair is supported on square tapering legs as seen in the above design.

for loo, two for whist, and one for quadrille one evening at Wanstead House. Entire fortunes were gambled away in an evening. With a roll of the dice and cut of the deck, all could be lost and men ruined. A games table featured a folding top, and doubled as a side table when not in use. Its inside was most often lined with baize and might be refined with wells for coins and candlestands.

The round tea table was an immensely practical and essential piece of furniture. Its tilt-top allowed it to take up less space, and its intimate size enabled it to be moved to the corner of a room easily. It was raised on a turned pedestal supported by cabriole-form legs and invariably made of mahogany. A smaller, shorter version was used as a kettle stand which supported the hot water for tea.

The English embrace of tea drinking resulted in a range of tea paraphernalia. In the early eighteenth century, tea superceded coffee and hot chocolate as the drink of choice. Exorbitantly expensive when it first arrived in England, its equipage was made of costly materials that reflected its exclusivity. Tea caddies contained two

Tripod tables, like this plum-pudding mahogany example, circa 1745, often have a bird-cage support underneath which allows the top to be tilted and placed flat against the wall when not in use.

This exceedingly rare triple-top walnut table, circa 1730, allowed its owner to indulge his passion for cards and tea. One leaf is veneered for taking tea, and the other has counter wells for gambling chips and has a baize-lined surface.

FAR RIGHT
This charming portrait painted by William Verelst in 1741 captures Sir Henry Gough, director of the East India Company, at home with his family. A porcelain teapot and tea cups sit next to an open tea caddy on the tripod table, and a silver kettle sits on a stand beside it.

The top of this mahogany and brass inlaid supper table in the manner of John Channon has several dished compartments designed to protect the tea paraphernalia.

Tea caddies, like this walnut example, were used to store costly tea leaves, and only the mistress of the house had its key.

FACING PAGE
Luxury items were always fashionably up-to-date, and tea caddies were no exception; an impressively varied collection is clustered together on a dumb-waiter in Bernard and Barbara Karr's sitting room.

Dorick Book Case. Plate

a Diameter

The influence of ancient temples on Palladian furniture is unmistakable in this 1739 design for a bookcase by Batty Langley.

FACING PAGE
The architectural character of this imposing mahogany breakfront bookcase is quintessentially Palladian.

receptacles for tea leaves along with a mixing bowl. They often had locks to safe-guard the valuable leaves from servants. While taking tea, the caddy would sit on the table, and so its appearance was always stylish and reflective of the wealth of its owner. Many Scottish games tables feature a frieze drawer that is fitted like a tea caddy, with space for tea-leaf compartments and a mixing bowl.

Existing forms of furniture were updated with the Palladian vocabulary of decoration. Bookcases and bureau bookcases in particular lent themselves to the

The fielded serpentine panels on this architectural mahogany cabinet-on-chest stray from Palladian classicism to the lively Rococo style.

FACING PAGE
A fitted interior of a scarlet japanned bureau bookcase is charmingly dressed with an assortment of porcelain objects in this sitting room by Brian J. McCarthy Associates.

application of an order and were surmounted by classical pediments, instead of the double dome. Columns, pilasters, and niches articulated the classical taste of its owner and bore testament to his education and refined taste.

ଔ ଔ ଔ

The classical style was trumpeted as providing the correct model for developing the newly rich and powerful nation's moral character and taste. Palladian villas were built according to classical principles to house souvenirs of the Grand Tour and furniture echoing the new taste with pillasters and pediments.

As important as creating a virtuous environment was a more comfortable one. The demands of fashionable society for an interior in which to comfortably entertain were met by innovations in furniture types and design. Tables and chairs were made to be portable and serve multiple functions, allowing a room to be used for dancing and playing cards. A taste for interiors that encouraged leisure and ease was soon acquired and pursued faithfully throughout the century.

ROCOCO FANTASIES

1745–1765

The ascendancy of the playful Rococo style was a brief interlude in British taste when the untamed and sublime natural world served as a model for beauty, and the example of the ancients was temporarily set aside. Even the conservative Palladian, Isaac Ware, ventured "to lead the student into all Fancy's wildness." French fashions once more dictated how to live, as well as how life should look.

Nobility and gentry mingled cheek by jowl at assemblies and balls and found the social ladder easier than ever to climb. As society continued to relax, interiors progressively became more organized around the idea of comfort and convenience. A new style of ornament emerged whose organic and whimsical character communicated the new emphasis on *l'art de vivre.*

Originating in France, the Rococo was composed of naturalistic ornament inspired by the grotto whose otherworldly ambiance so fascinated society for thousands of years that man-made versions were created. Ornament of rockwork, stalactites, shells, and the like were arranged asymmetrically to achieve a spontaneous effect. The lively spirit that imbued Rococo decoration mirrored the contemporary frivolity in society, where duchesses dressed up as milkmaids, and the novel first made its appearance. At the time, it was described as the "modern" taste, and contemporary critics deemed it decidedly anti-classical. In contrast to the Palladian style, painters, sculptors, and craftsmen were the innovators of this picturesque style, not architects.

Grotesque scrollwork dominated Baroque design and was ideal for incorporating rocaille (rockwork or grottowork) decoration; its interlacing arabesques were now reimagined in three dimensions and easily incorporated chinoiserie and Gothic ornament. French painters and designers such as Claude Audran III, his pupil Antoine Watteau, and Pierre Le Pautre played a pivotal role in evolving the grotesque by introducing such Rococo elements as "flowers, birds, and an infinite number of other whimsies, which make a most agreeable effect." In France, where this fanciful ornamentation first reached its fullest expression in the 1720s and 1730s, all elements of a room from paneling to chimneypieces were conceived in the new fashion.

89

Charles-Nicolas Cochin (French, 1688–1754) after Gilles-Marie Oppenord (French, 1672–1742), Design for a Tapestry from a set Dedicated to the Seasons, 1720–30. Etching on off-white laid paper. Cooper-Hewitt National Design Museum, Smithsonian Institution.

This exquisite design incorporates Rococo decoration, including C-scrolls, falling water, interlace, and naturalistic ornament.

FACING PAGE
Britannia herself presides over this beautifully executed giltwood mirror, circa 1760.

Although England had a more tentative relationship with the new style than the rest of Europe and would always label it "French," new attitudes toward what constituted beauty made the English increasingly receptive to it. For the Palladians, mathematically calculated proportions taken from nature and applied systematically had been the aesthetically correct path to beauty. Now philosophers and artists looked to the outdoors itself and embraced its variety and irregularity. Influenced by the Chinese concept of "sharawaggi," the beauty of unstudied irregularity, flowers, trees, and shrubs were purposely planned in their gardens to appear in natural disarray, instead of topiaries and other vegetation arranged in geometric patterns of formal gardens which had dominated landscape design throughout the seventeenth century. Follies and artificial grottoes were scattered throughout as necessary accessories for a fashionable garden and the ha-ha, a sunken boundary, replaced perimeter walls and allowed views to extend beyond the garden into the fields and forests. This intended disorder correlated to the asymmetry of the Rococo, as well as to the preference for flowers and foliage as decoration over columns and arches.

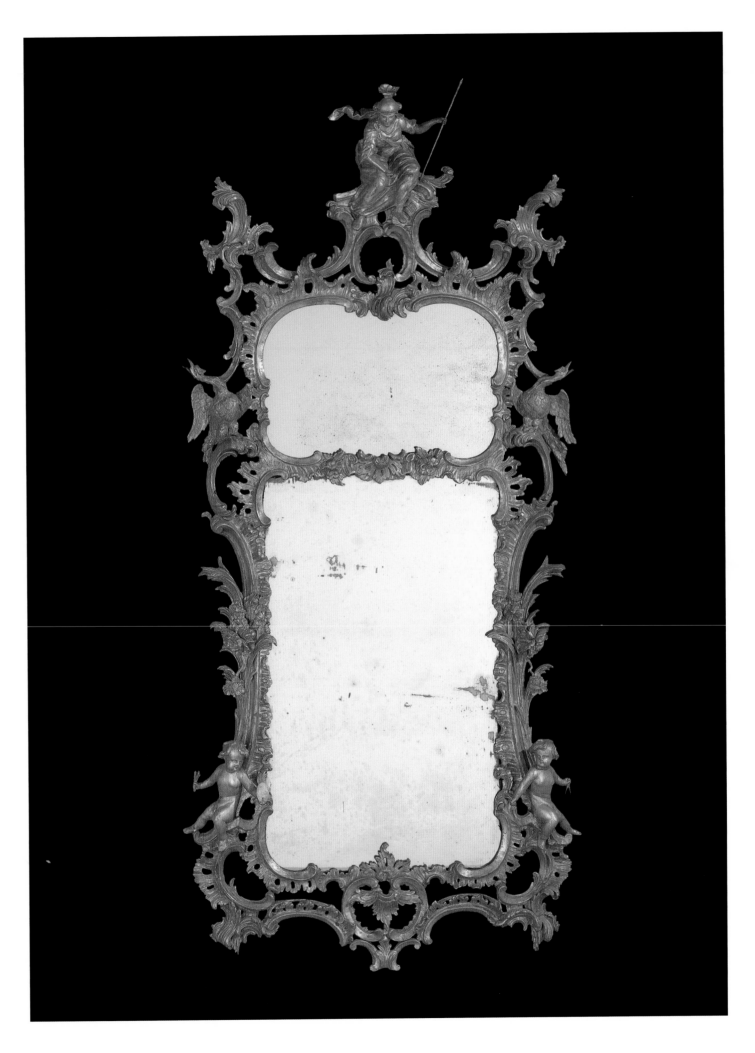

THE ROCOCO INTERIOR

The imposing reception rooms of the International Court and Palladian styles designed solely to overwhelm visitors were completely outmoded by this time. More spaces were devoted to private pursuits, not public entertainments, and were designated with particular purposes, such as libraries, music rooms, and dining rooms. The decoration and furnishings of these rooms received individual treatment to create a variety of different environments. The new emphasis on privacy also led to the creation of backstairs and passageways for servants who were now concealed as much as possible.

The state bedchamber was gradually cut off from the rest of the apartment, leaving a circuit of reception rooms arranged around a central staircase with the state bedchamber and its dressing room and closet off to the side. This was the standard for the London houses of the aristocracy and was gradually adopted for their country houses as well. Drawing rooms by this time were completely unattached to a bedchamber and association with a person's apartment. As people spent more time in the common rooms and less in their own, the size of rooms adjusted accordingly. Dressing rooms became larger than the bedroom and were used as private sitting rooms.

In contrast to the uniformity of exteriors which still followed Palladian design, options for the decoration of interior spaces became more varied and whimsical during the Rococo period. Walls, for example, could be painted, hung with textiles or wallpaper, or incorporate Rococo motifs into wall paneling. Applied in plaster or even papier-mâché, wall decoration supplanted the more sober wainscot and architectural pillars and pediments as a fashionable wall treatment. The malleable quality of plaster encouraged extravagant Rococo fantasies to inhabit the wall and become works of art in themselves.

Wallpaper was immensely popular by mid-century and available at many prices. Most imitated fashionable textiles: damasks, velvets, chintzes, and even needlepoint. Flock wallpaper was intensely fashionable and rivaled in price the cut velvet it emulated. Paper hand painted with trees, birds, and flowers imported from China was also highly desirable and very expensive. It was sold in sheets and was

Decorator Brian J. McCarthy dresses a richly carved mahogany bed, circa 1755, with crisp white linens.

FACING PAGE
Nineteenth-century European paintings are stacked above an important japanned pagoda-top cabinet, circa 1760, which is virtually identical to the famous chinoiserie cabinets made by the Linnells for Badminton House.

FOLLOWING PAGES
The state bedchamber at Nostell Priory is appointed with handpainted Chinese wallpaper and furniture by Thomas Chippendale.

pasted directly on the wall or onto canvas secured by battens. Sheets printed with various decoration were available for purchase and could be cut up and applied to walls in all sorts of combinations. Entire rooms were covered with engravings and made into "print-rooms." For a simpler look, ready-made paint was available for sale by mid-century, and many rooms were painted by homeowners themselves for the first time, with the aid of specialist painters.

Wall hangings remained fashionable, with textile patterns changing according to the fashion of the day. Curtains were made of the same upholstery as the wall hangings and bed hangings. The most fashionable windows were dressed with divided curtains, pulled up on the diagonal. Unlike the early eighteenth century, the hanging curtains didn't simply hang down, but gathered in festoons by pulleys. Pull-up curtains also had festoons, with fixed tails on the sides.

The stylish home covered its wood floors with wall to wall carpets. Isaac Ware, whose architectural designs were studied widely, wrote in 1754 that "the use of carpeting at this time has set aside the ornamenting of floors in a great measure." Strips of carpet were sewn together with a decorative border around the perimeter. Carpets woven at the Wilton carpet factory in Wiltshire with a cut-pile were the most expensive and used in the best rooms. Oriental carpets (often referred to as Turkey carpets) were imported in large quantities. Floor cloths made of glazed canvas were frequently used under dining-room tables to catch crumbs. Most were painted with geometric patterns, but some were intricately decorated in bold colors.

A renewed dedication to the "Chinese taste" emerged and informed the furnishing of interiors as well as garden planning. As one Englishman said in 1756:

> . . . Nay, so excessive is the love of Chinese architecture become, that at present foxhunters would be sorry to break a leg in pursuing their sport in leaping any gate that was not made in the eastern taste of little bits of wood standing in all directions.

Bedchambers and ladies' dressing rooms were the most common candidates for an overall chinoiserie treatment, but it occasionally crept into the larger reception rooms as well. Thomas Chippendale, one of the most renowned purveyors of furniture of the time, described his Chinese-style chairs in *The Gentleman and Cabinet-Maker's Director* as "very popular for a lady's dressing-room: especially if it is hung with India paper. They will likewise suit Chinese temples [outbuildings in the gardens]." He called the Chinese taste "the most useful of any other," that is, the most fashionable.

The turrets and crockets of the "Gothick" style were also folded into the Rococo mix as the library became a staple of a gentleman's house. The cabinet had once been sufficient to contain his treasured books, but soon the rise of the antiquarian and the amassing of quantities of books called for another solution. Long galleries were planned with bookcases in the early eighteenth century, but soon dedicated libraries furnished to increase the comfort and enjoyment of study were the rule. Books on architecture, natural history and botany, politics, philosophy, literature, music, and genealogy filled the bookcases in a typical gentleman's library. Busts of philosophers, globes, telescopes, and scientific instruments also bore testament to their owners' devotion to study. Collections of old-master drawings and sketches were stowed in boxes, taken out occasionally to muse over with guests.

The gentlemanly pursuits of studying and reading were associated with antiquarianism. Gothic decoration, in turn, harkened back to its early British architectural origins, and was felt to be a proper way to appoint the library. Bookcases and chairs were enriched with Gothic spires, arches, and quatrefoils. Horace Walpole, statesman and acerbic social observer, was one of the main proponents of this fashion, and went one step further by building an entire house in the 1750s, Strawberry Hill, in Twickenham, in the Gothic style complete with suitable furnishings. He collaborated with craftsmen to create bookcases and chimneypieces based on medieval tombs and choir screens.

It wasn't a slavish copy of medieval furniture that furnished Walpole's Strawberry Hill or the libraries of his contemporaries. As he remarked:

> My closet is as perfect in its way as the library; and it would be difficult to suspect that it had not been a remnant of the ancient convent, only newly painted and gilt. My cabinet, nay, nor house, convey any conception; every true Goth must perceive that they are more the works of fancy than of imitation.

Gothic decoration was adapted most commonly for the library, as the one at Strawberry Hill demonstrates, as it was thought to complement studying and other antiquarian pursuits.

Strawberry Hill was transformed into "a little Gothic castle" between 1747 and 1792 by Horace Walpole. The gallery, seen here, was the most spectacular room in the house— "all Gothicism and gold, and crimson and looking-glass."

Moreover, no one was interested in sacrificing the comfort of modern furniture for fashion, so Gothic decoration, such as the ogee arch, a pointed arch formed by two reverse curves, cluster columns, pinnacles with crockets, and tracery was playfully applied to current furniture forms. Because Walpole's Strawberry Hill was an anomaly, visitors flocked to see this curiosity. A resurgence of interest in the Gothic Revival was felt at the end of the century when such arbiters of taste as the Prince Regent and William Beckford built entirely in the Gothic idiom.

Drawing Books and the Furniture Trade

A much more conservative version of the Rococo took root in England than on the Continent. Rocaille first appeared in silver and engravings for ornament in the 1730s and gained currency slowly. The St. Martin's Lane Academy, which taught fine artists and artisans the latest techniques and styles, was one of its main proponents and influential in disseminating the modern Rococo style to its pupils, which included workmen in the studios of goldsmiths and furniture makers.

A desire for furniture incorporating this decoration followed the publication of Matthias Lock's *New Drawing Book of Ornaments, Shields, Compartments, Masks, etc.* in 1740, the first English drawing book of furniture in the Rococo style. Lock was from a family of carvers and joiners and established himself as an exceptional designer and craftsman in the 1740s with the publication of several books of designs.

Matthias Lock's published designs were among the first to depict Rococo-style furniture. A whirling dervish of foliate-scrolls, animals, and floral sprays combine in a 1746 engraving of a table by Lock.

FACING PAGE
This spectacular giltwood mirror (originally from a pair), circa 1745, is an example of the earliest furniture in Britain executed in the Rococo taste. The employment of intricate and tight decoration as well as heavy and bold carving and the use of bearded terms are all Lock signatures.

A Design for a Chimney Piece

T. Chippendale inv.t et delin.

Published according to Act 1761.

M. Darly sculp.

The importance of variety and invention in the conception of Rococo design can not be stressed enough and led to a profusion of printed designs from which to choose. Design books included instructions on perspective and drawing to help craftsmen invent their own designs, not merely follow others. Many craftsmen felt the need for a state-supported school that would nurture home-grown design. John Gwyn wrote in his *Essay on Design, including proposals for erecting a Public Academy to be supported by Voluntary Subscription* in 1749:

> All Men whose Employment is in the fashioning of Earth, Wood, Metal, or Stone, or in ornamenting the various Utensils of Life which are fashioned from these, must acknowledge that Drawing turns greatly to their Account; and that if they can form no Designs of their own, they are constantly obliged to copy those of better Artists.

The designer Thomas Johnson's *150 New Designs* published in 1758 were among the most influential in England. Johnson borrowed heavily from Continental engravings to produce the most extravagant and capricious drawings for Rococo-style furniture. However, it is Thomas Chippendale's *The Gentleman and Cabinet-Maker's Director*—"as being calculated to assist the one in the Choice, and the other in the Execution of the Designs"—whose success has endured to this day and secured Chippendale's place foremost in the pantheon of well-know designers and cabinetmakers of this period. *The Director* was first published in 1754 and reissued twice with amendments.

Although he was a leading London cabinetmaker and produced exquisitely made furniture, it is important to understand that Chippendale did not make with his own hands most of the furniture that came out of his workshop, which was located in St. Martin's, the center of London's fine-furniture trade and close to St. Martin's Lane Academy. Rather, he was an entrepreneur who ran a full-service business; he supplied in addition to furniture, curtains, carpets, wallpapers, and even coffins to a clientele of noble- and gentlemen. A German visitor to the West End of

London commented in 1767, "the master himself no longer touches a tool. Instead he oversees the work of his forty journeymen."

Chippendale's designs were not innovations but depictions of the latest fashions, and many have labeled furniture from this period as "Chippendale" to the dismay of furniture historians. *The Director* had more influence on provincial cabinetmakers than those established in London, who weren't in need of a guide to what was fashionable. Copies of his designs traveled to the English provinces, and as far away as America, Portugal, and India. At least nine copies of his *Director* were recorded in North America as of 1786.

The design books published by Chippendale and his peers establish for the first time an understanding of the different workshops and cabinetmakers in London, whereas the identity of fine furniture makers before this time is usually unknown. Equally, there were many fine cabinetmakers who never published their designs and accordingly are less widely known today. Other leading London cabinetmakers were William Vile who completed commissions for George III and Queen Charlotte, John Cobb, William and John Linnell, and William Ince and John Mayhew, the latter of which also published a book of designs. Many smaller firms also existed that offered more specialist services or were subcontracted by the larger firms.

As the number of workshops grew, competition heightened. To captivate clients, luxurious permanent stores stocked with ready-made wares became common. Another way to distinguish one's wares from those in another shop was to vary the design and create an item that was one of a kind, hence the importance of having the skills to create one's own designs.

The role of the upholsterer became extremely important as padded chairs and curtains became necessary luxuries. A new homeowner in London wrote in 1747:

> I have just finished my House, and must now think of furnishing it with fashionable Furniture. The Upholder is chief Agent in this Case: He is the Man upon whose Judgment I rely in the Choice of Goods; and I suppose he has not only Judgment in the Materials, but Taste in the Fashions, and Skill in the Workmanship. This Trademan's Genius must be universal in every Branch of Furniture; though his proper Craft is to fit up Beds, Window-Curtains, Hangings, and to cover Chairs that have stuffed Bottoms: He was originally a Species of the Taylor; but, by degrees, has crept over his Head, and set up as Connoisieur [sic] in every Article that belongs to a House."

"A Systematical Order of Raffle Leaf from the Line of Beauty," a plate from The Universal System of Household Furniture *by William Ince and John Mayhew, 1759. Foliate C-scrolls like this one were the foundation of many Rococo concoctions, particularly mirrors.*

Furniture

Nor custom stale Her infinite variety.

—WILLIAM SHAKESPEARE, *Antony and Cleopatra*, Act 2, Scene 3

"Infinite Variety" are the two words that "sum'd up all the charms of beauty," according to William Hogarth in his 1753 treatise *Analysis of Beauty* and were the guiding principles for cabinetmakers in the mid-eighteenth century. Its physical manifestation was the serpentine line called by Hogarth the line of beauty and grace which "by its waving and winding at the same time different ways, leads the eye in a pleasing manner along the continuity of its variety." Accompanying illustrations compared the curves of a landscape to those of cabriole chair legs.

This mahogany marble-top side table (above, and detail at left), circa 1765, is executed directly from plate LIV of Chippendale's Director *and appeared in all three editions. Furniture in a generalized* Director *style is relatively common, but such precise replication of a published design is extremely rare.*

French Commode Table

The French commode, seen here in a Chippendale design, was an extremely grand chest of drawers in the new Rococo style.

Translated into mahogany, the serpentine line was expressed in the undulating fronts of chests and commodes, and shaped tops and seat rails of chairs, in addition to the cabriole leg. The ubiquitous C-scrolls and S-scrolls that were the foundation of the Rococo grotesque both derived from the serpentine.

Furniture served as an ideal outlet for the sculptural aspects of the Rococo. Many of the French printmakers, whose engravings of this ornament found their way to England, were craftsmen who worked with three-dimensional surfaces. Carvers were able to show off their skill, and carving became the most desired and highly-paid specialist technique.

> There is not a bed, table, a chair, or even a grate, that is not twisted into so many ridiculous and grotesque figures, and so decorated with the heads, beaks, wings and claws of birds and beasts, that Milton's 'Gorgons and hydra and chimeras dire', are not to be compared with them.

The almost exclusive use of mahogany by this time made it possible for furniture to be rigorously carved and remain sturdy, such as in the fashionable, highly wrought chair backs and Chinese fretwork (a trellis-form ornament) decoration. Mahogany

Exotic calamander banding distinguishes this serpentine mahogany commode, circa 1760.

imported from Cuba was found to possess a variety of interesting figures, unlike that from San Domingo which had a very straight grain. "Plum-pudding" or "fiddle-back" cuts of veneer have a beautiful dappled appearance, where as "flame" or "crotch" mahogany were large-sized, dramatic veneers used to their best advantage on the doors of cabinet pieces.

Side tables and mirrors were particularly well-suited to the more vigorous expressions of the Rococo. Pier glasses and side tables, or commodes, were often designed en suite and were displayed in drawing rooms and the best bedrooms. Commodes were extremely grand chests of drawers or cabinets designed in the new style whose name referred to its French source. They were not, as in America, meant to store chamberpots. The traditional plain chest of drawers changed little. Now made mostly out of mahogany, they featured cockbeading, a molding applied to the edges of drawer fronts, and bracket feet, which were made of two pieces of wood joining at the corner, with an arch or curve shape cut out of the front piece. A taste for taller chests of drawers developed mid-century, and examples with five or six drawers were available. Chests-on-chests, sometimes called tallboys, evolved similarly.

Giltwood mirror frames, free from the limitations of mahogany, were most able to live out the wild fantasies of Rococo designers. Interconnecting broken scrolls

The masterful carving of English Rococo furniture is on display in this bedroom by Ralph Harvard.

Thomas Johnson's designs, such as this 1755 example of a girandole, are among the most fantastical and exaggerated of the English Rococo.

RIGHT
The small scale and freedom of girandoles from structural require-ments encouraged the use of extravagant ornament, as implied by their name: the term "girandole" is taken from the Italian girandola, *a type of firecracker.*

Masterfully carved C-scrolls and floral sprays embellish this grand George III giltwood mirror, circa 1760, which is enlarged with the addition of border plates.

mingled C-scrolls and S-scrolls with rockwork and chinoiserie elements such as ho-ho birds and pagoda crestings. Girandoles and wall brackets became extremely desirable, and, like mirrors, were often designed in the shape that epitomized Rococo's love of asymmetry: the cartouche. Overmantel mirrors ran riot with brackets to support porcelain and whimsical figures of mandarins and pagods.

Candles were used liberally for illumination and a larger number of candelabra executed in metals and crystal were made. Candlestands were used in the best rooms, but placed in the corners. Executed sympathetically with the rest of an interior's furnishings, they were japanned, gilt, or carved mahogany.

Many fashionable homes took advantage of the advances in upholstery and ordered cushy armchairs for their favorite rooms. The Louis Quinze armchair with curvaceous lines and ample padding was considered the ultimate in comfort and style, and many designs for its English incarnation, "the French Chair" were published in Chippendale's *Director* and other books. However, most English chairs featured rectilinear backs and seats which prevented the domed stuffing with rounded edges the French were able to use. Like all chairs, these were arranged against the wall when not in use, and a less expensive fabric was used for the back.

RIGHT

Graceful proportions and fine turning distinguish this pair of deceptively simple mahogany candlestands, circa 1765

FACING PAGE

This giltwood overmantel mirror, circa 1760, is an extraordinary example of the period's penchant for chinoiserie.

FACING PAGE TOP
The ample padding and curves of the
French chair, as illustrated by Chippendale,
was the ultimate in comfort.

FACING PAGE BOTTOM
This exceptionally large pair of walnut
library armchairs, circa 1760, are
taken after a French chair design
by Chippendale.

ABOVE
Delightful needlework depicting
European court figures on this pair
of walnut armchairs, circa 1755,
communicates the lighthearted spirit
of the Rococo.

The interlaced backs of this pair of mahogany armchairs, circa 1760, after the 1741 designs of William de la Cour capture the transition between the Queen Anne hooped-back chairs with vasiform backsplat to the intricately carved and varied back popularized by Chippendale's Director.

Three designs for a side chair from Chippendale's Director *provide cabinetmakers with several options.*

Slipcovers made of linen were frequently used for the most lavishly upholstered seat furniture and removed when entertaining.

The main innovation in the wooden chairback is the enormous variety of ornament used. The solid urn-shaped backsplat of Queen Anne chairs became divided into flat interlacing loops or straps, and embellished with fanciful ornament such as ribbons, cabochons, and fretwork. In general, although pierced and incorporating additional decoration, the backsplat retained the urn or vase shape. The uprights, the outermost part of the chair back, are vertical, and the top rail of the chair back is of serpentine shape with the ends twisting upward. The cabriole leg continued its long

A mahogany side chair, circa 1760, supported on beautifully scrolling legs is pulled up to a bureau bookcase in this bedroom designed by Ralph Harvard.

BELOW

The importance of variety to eighteenth-century taste promoted the incorporation of an extensive vocabulary of ornament, such as the drapery and tassel decoration seen on this mahogany armchair, circa 1745.

FACING PAGE

The tall, interlaced chair backs made famous by the designs of Chippendale continue to be the most popular style for dining, as seen here in this charming chinoiserie-themed dining room.

ABOVE

The geometric, open backs of this set of black japanned chairs, circa 1770, are extrapolated from Chinese railing or fretwork, which became extremely fashionable in the 1750s when a magnificent but short-lived "Chinese Bridge" was built across the river Thames at Hampton Court.

RIGHT

The style of this set of mahogany chairs, circa 1760, is often referred to as "Cockpen" and "Chinese Chippendale" and remains incredibly popular.

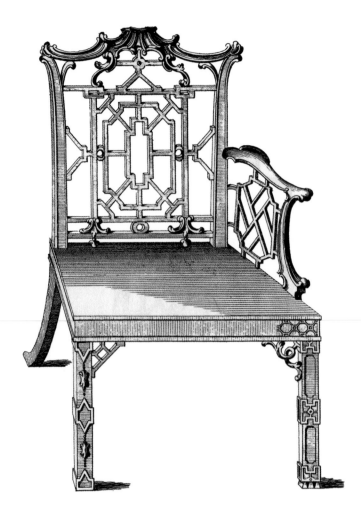

Chippendale deemed this Chinese chair design "very proper for a Lady's Dressing Room: especially if it is hung with India Paper."

run of popularity, and usually terminated in the claw and ball or scroll-form foot. The straight square leg, which would soon eclipse the cabriole, was used exclusively for Chinese and Gothic style chairs.

Chinese chairs are still incredibly popular and today are often referred to as "Chinese Chippendale" after the design for Chinese chairs published in Chippendale's *Director*, or as "Cockpen," reputedly after chairs of this design in the Earl of Dalhousie's family pew in the village church of Cockpen, a settlement in Midlothian, Scotland. The legs are straight and the back is square with open lattice-work. Often fretwork, carved in low relief on the legs, and a pagoda-form top rail were further refinements. These chairs were often made of mahogany or lacquered wood.

Gothic chairs had the same basic form as Chinese chairs—both had square backs and straight legs. However, instead of open-fretwork backs, arches inspired from the tracery on Gothic windows are used, as well as crockets and pierced quatrefoils.

The massive side tables of William Kent contradicted the new playful spirit and a lighter, restrained version entered the drawing room and saloon. Friezes are carved and the legs are cabriole, or straight in Gothic and Chinese variations. Marble tops were still in demand. Card tables, made in great quantities, followed suit.

The British taste for tea ran unabated, and in 1745, a contributor to *The Female Spectator* wrote: "The tea table costs more to support than it would to maintain two

Similar to the Chinese style of chair with straight legs and fretwork back, the pointed arches and tracery on this pair of mahogany armchairs, circa 1760, from Coley Hill House, make this model decisively Gothic.

Cluster columns derived from Gothic stonework support this mahogany side table, circa 1770, worthy of Strawberry Hill.

FACING PAGE
A striking giltwood Gothic overmantel mirror, circa 1760, holds its own in this jewel box of a room by Billy Francis.

children at nurse." More elaborate versions of tea tables were devised, called "china-tables" by Chippendale. These featured a rectangular top surmounted by a gallery, often fretted, which protected the tea paraphernalia from falling. Round tripod tables also began having galleried tops.

Pembroke tables make their first appearance in the 1750s, and were used as elegant, convenient tables for meals taken alone. Plate LIII of the first edition of *The Director* illustrates such a table with drop-leaves supported by brackets, which Chippendale describes as a breakfast table. Its name is reputedly taken from that "of the lady who first gave orders for one of them, and who probably gave the first idea of such a table"—perhaps the Countess of Pembroke.

The necessity for large pedestal library tables grew along with the increase of dedicated libraries. A large leather-lined writing surface generally of rectangular shape is supported on two pedestals which are fitted with drawers, folio slides, or however else the client desired. Extremely large ones were made to be used on both sides and earned the name "partner's" desk. Carrying handles are sometimes found on the side of the pedestals encouraging portability. Patrons were able to tailor desks to suit their needs: it could be fitted with all manner of drawers, cupboards, folio slides, etc. Chippendale's *Director* demonstrates the escalating demand for these library tables: the third edition includes plates for eleven examples in contrast to six in the first edition.

Bookcases, of course, were more important than ever. The most important development of this period is the addition of "wings" to the center cabinet. The largest examples often were of breakfront form, in which the center piece projects past the wings. Rococo, chinoiserie, and Gothic decoration were applied to the pediment, moldings on cabinet doors, and glazing bars of the upper section. The bureau bookcase absorbed these stylistic changes, but otherwise altered little. Display cabinets, with glazed upper sections, used mainly to show off cherished china gained currency, and, in form, are often indiscernible from bookcases. Fretwork, japanning, and other chinoiserie decoration was often suitably used on such pieces.

FACING PAGE
A side table with Gothic fretwork and straight legs, circa 1765, adheres to the severe lines of this Neoclassical interior at Stanmer Park.

A pair of mahogany card tables, circa 1760, have beautifully carved legs (detail) enriched with rocaille cabochons and foliate C-scrolls.

A Gothic Fret for Friezes &c

A Chinese Fret proper for Cabinet Makers &c

*Fretwork could incorporate Gothic
or chinoiserie tracery, as shown in
the design here.*

*Detail of a blind fretwork frieze from
a mahogany side table, circa 1765.*

*Spectacular pierced Chinese fretwork
enriches every element of this mahogany
silver or "china" table, circa 1765.*

Small-scale and finished on all sides, the pembroke table is perfect for placing a lamp near a favorite chair, as Cullman and Kravis have done here.

The "serpentine line of beauty" graces the top of this high-style tripod table, circa 1760, complete with a pierced protective gallery.

Pembroke tables, such as this version from Littlecote House, were often used for taking meals. The father of one of Jane Austen's heroines used a "small-sized Pembroke, on which two of his daily meals had, for forty years been crowded."

ABOVE
This rare telescopic mahogany reading stand, circa 1750, most likely served as a useful aid to the antiquarian studies of its owner.

ABOVE RIGHT
From every side, one can enjoy the serpentine line of this mahogany partners' desk, circa 1770.

RIGHT
Almost without exception, library furniture was made exclusively out of mahogany, respected for its deep color and strength.

FACING PAGE
King George III's fascination with books led to his desire to form a new library worthy of a monarch. It culminated in the purpose-built Octagon Library at the Queen's House (now Buckingham Palace), which is furnished with the requisite pedestal desk.

A Chinese black lacquer bureau bookcase, circa 1750, is made for export after English designs.

Irish Furniture

There are many admirers of eighteenth-century Irish furniture who are drawn to its quirkiness and individuality. Despite its growing popularity, there is little published information available, leaving much as uncharted terrain. For some years now, auction houses have been prone to attribute anything atypical as "possibly Irish." In general though, furniture made in Ireland followed English designs closely, with distinct regional preferences emerging. Because of the time it took for fashions to crossover, Irish furniture fashions lagged behind London and retained some of the Kentian heaviness. Irish side tables and case pieces, for example, have heavier proportions than their English counterparts. Friezes on side tables are commonly much deeper.

Rococo and classical ornament were often thrown together in a whimsical, quirky way, as seen on some of the side tables featured here. The hairy paw foot was frequently used to finish legs, and the eagle was a popular armrest termination—both remnants from the Palladian style. Carving is also heavier and at times exuberantly outsized, or, conversely, is executed in low relief, in imitation of the gilt gesso work found on Queen Anne pieces.

ೞ ೞ ೞ

The high value placed on whimsy and individuality by mid-eighteenth-century English society pushed artisans to produce the most sumptuous and varied items for

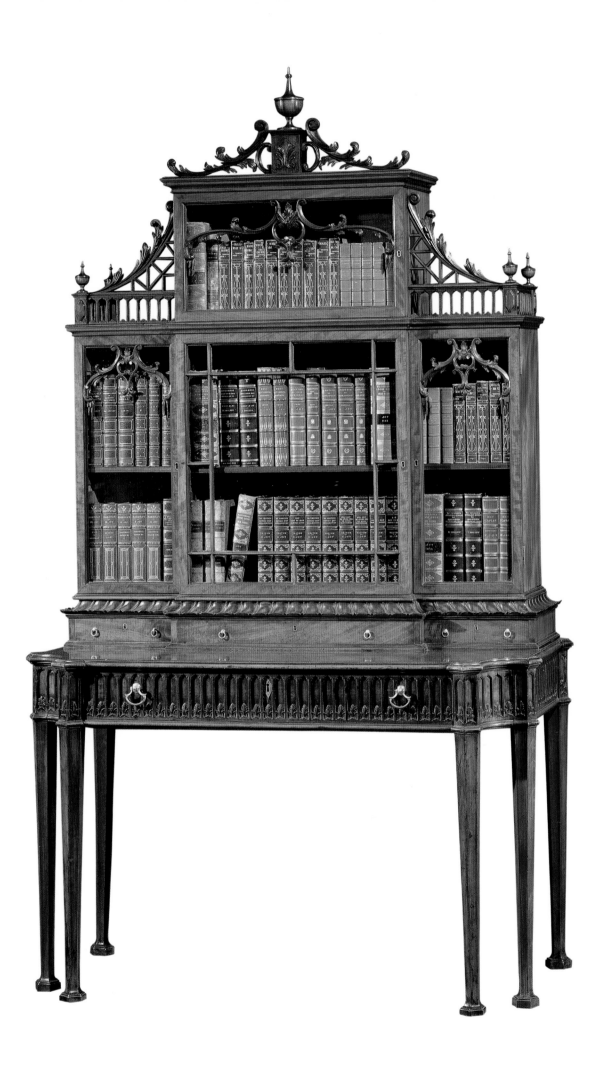

This mahogany side table, circa 1750, incorporates typically Irish traits, such as flat carving, "broken" cabriole legs ending in pinched paw feet, and, most of all, the splendidly silly mock-ferocious lion mask.

ABOVE

The grotesque mask carved on the frieze of this Irish mahogany side table, circa 1750, was popular in Ireland and was inspired from stone examples dating to the Celtic period.

The low-relief carving on this mahogany Irish double-chairback sette, circa 1745, derives from gilt gessowork decoration. The eagle head armrest terminals were another favored Irish device.

This mahogany bureau bookcase, circa 1760, displays many characteristics of eighteenth-century Irish furniture made in Dublin. The engaged, fluted columns of the upper section, the repertoire of moldings, the scalloped pediment, and profile of the bracket feet are found in many documented examples.

consumption available than ever before. Eager to capture the custom of a demanding clientele in an increasingly competitive market, leading cabinetmakers studied the latest fashions from France and were able to invent their own to suit the tastes of any customer.

As the English overdosed on Rococo, designers and craftsmen scrambled to find something new to arouse the excitement of their patrons. The original bluestocking, Elizabeth Montague, moaned:

> . . . sick of Grecian elegance and symmetry, or Gothic grandeur and magnificence, we must all seek the barbarous gaudy gout of the Chinese; and fat-headed Pagods, and shaking Mandarins, bear the prize from the finest works of antiquity; and Apollo and Venus must give way to a big fat idol with a sconce on his head.

Apollo and Venus didn't have to step into the background for long. Ironically, it was the classical world that provided fresh inspiration, translated by the architect and interior decorator Robert Adam who ventured "to transfuse the beautiful spirit of antiquity with novelty and variety."

THE NEOCLASSICAL STYLE

THE AGE OF ROBERT ADAM
1765–1790

The massive entablature, the ponderous compartment ceiling, the tabernacle frame, almost the only species of ornament formerly known, in the country, are now universally exploded, and in their place, we have adopted a beautiful variety of light moldings, gracefully formed, delicately enriched and arranged with propriety and skill.

—ROBERT AND JAMES ADAM, *The Works in Architecture*

In 1773 Robert and James Adam published *The Works in Architecture*, perhaps one of the most influential and innovative collection of complete designs for buildings and interiors in British design history. In this tome, Robert Adam introduced a new confectionary style of elaborate classical ornament applied skillfully and gracefully to every surface imaginable, all intricately designed to coordinate harmoniously.

Adam's experiences on the Grand Tour as well as copious new publications depicting classical remains provided ample fodder for these designs. The current craze for Greek vases and their airy linear decoration were even more influential to the development of Adam's style. Rococo shapes were reigned in, proportions lightened, and in so doing Adam offered his countrymen a version of Neoclassicism that was volumes more playful and inventive than the rigid, static Palladian model.

The ability of Adam to direct the taste of his time reflected the ascendancy of the architect. The court of Saint James had long since been two steps behind the times and had given way to the cultivated nobility of the country decades before to decide what was fashionable. But in the latter half of the eighteenth century, even the supremely confident aristocrat depended upon his architect to dream up entire rooms, from ceiling to carpet to pier mirror. Adam's meticulous attention to detail and the designs of interior schemes in his *Works* were crucial to this development and made the volume one of his greatest contributions to interior decoration. Daniel Marot and William Kent had also done this, but nowhere near to the extent of Adam who attended to the design of even the smallest elements of room down to the doorknobs.

Girandoles in the first Drawing room
Girandoles dans la première Salle d'Assemblée

Curtain Cornice of the Bed Chamber
Corniche aux Rideaux de la Chambre à coucher

N.º I.

Curtain Cornice of the Etruscan room
Corniche aux Rideaux de la Chambre Étrusque

Plate VIII.

Girandole in
the Nich of the
Etruscan room

Girandole dans la
Niche de la
Chambre Étrusque

Girandoles in the
Etruscan room

Girandoles dans la
Chambre Étrusque

Folding Doors of the third Drawing room
Portes à deux Battens pour la troisieme Salle d'Assemblée

Folding Doors for the Etruscan room
Portes à deux Battens pour la Chambre Étrusque

Top of a Commode in the Countess of Derby's
Dressing room

Dessus d'une Commode dans la Chambre à Toilette
de Mad.ᵐᵉ la Comtesse de Derby

Front of a Commode in the Countess of Derby's
Dressing room

Facade d'une Commode dans la Chambre
à Toilette de Mad.ᵐᵉ la Comtesse de Derby

R.ᵗ Adam Architect 1774.

Scale of

Published as the Act directs 1777.

feet

B. Pastorini incidit.

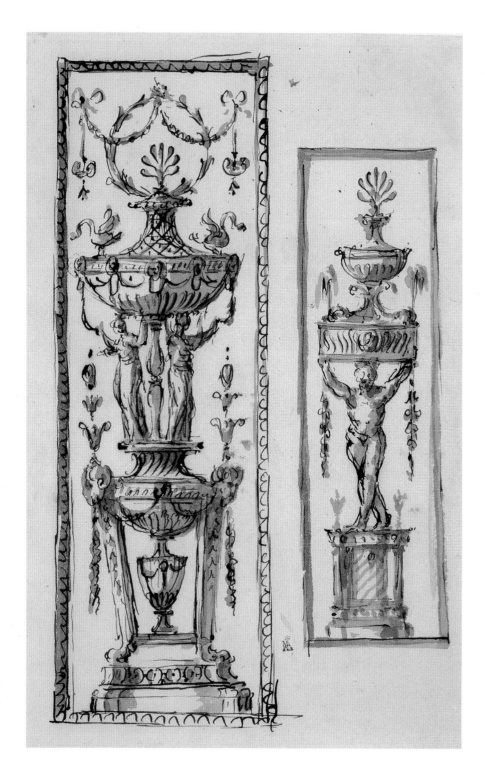

These sketched designs for ornate panels by Robert Adam illustrate how he interlaced classical ornament, such as urns and anthemia, with husk garlands.

Style was now piloted by architects and their dominant position in society as tastemakers was noted by all. "Father of English Potters" and savvy businessman Josiah Wedgwood recognized this and wrote to his partner that "we were really unfortunate in the introduction of our jasper into public notice, that we could not prevail upon the architects to be godfathers to our child."

Born in 1728 in Fife, Scotland, to an architect, Adam worked closely with his brothers James and John, leading some to say the style was more of a family effort. In addition to armfuls of talent, the members of the Adam family were canny marketers and experts at extolling their own capabilities. While in Rome on his Grand Tour, Robert met the important architect and designer Piranesi whose drawing style so

impressed him, he delayed his travels to study under Piranesi's tutelage. The Italian artist's dictum, "It is not the multiplicity of ornaments that offends the eyes of the spectator, but the bad disposition," was certainly taken to heart by Adam who will never be accused of minimalism, and whose signature arrangements of interlacing classical ornament were extremely elaborate and detailed. However, his complex designs were sometimes more successful on paper than in execution: Horace Walpole, on seeing the state bed at Osterley Park designed by Adam, commented, "What would Vitruvius think of a dome decorated by a milliner?" However ornate and intricate, Adam's designs offered a version of Neoclassicism that was an antidote to the anti-classical Rococo whose lack of rules and unpredictability had made many uncomfortable.

The state bed at Osterley Park designed by Robert Adam in 1776 was conceived as a Temple of Venus with elements taken from Stuart and Revett's Antiquities of Athens. *Horace Walpole, however, commented that it was "too theatric and too like a modern Headdress."*

CLASSICAL INFLUENCES

FACING PAGE
Charles Townley proudly displays his famous collection of ancient statuary in his gallery in this painting by Johann Zoffany. He is seated on a bergere while reading at a pembroke table.

The great debate amongst European tastemakers in the second half of the eighteenth century wasn't whether to emulate the example of antiquity but whether to imitate the classical precedents of the Greeks or the Romans. The excavations of Pompeii and Herculaneum, both ancient Roman cities frozen in time by the eruption of Mount Vesuvius in AD 79, fueled the contemporary fascination with classical art. The Society of the Dilettanti, founded in 1732 as a club for British gentlemen who had been on the Grand Tour, sponsored many trips abroad to explore the great ancient ruins, which resulted in important books of engraved drawings, such as Robert Wood's *The Ruins of Palmyra* in 1753 and James "Athenian" Stuart and Nicholas Revett's *Antiquities of Athens* in 1762.

The supremacy of Greek art was gradually acknowledged. The noted art historian Johann Winckelmann's *Reflections on the Imitation of Greek Works in Painting and Sculpture* published in 1755, and available in English in 1765, was exceptionally persuasive and convinced many that "The only way for us to become great lies in the imitation of the Greeks." Greece had not commonly been on the Grand Tour as it was thought to be too primitive and dangerous, and these new books of engravings depicting Greek ruins were pivotal in circulating the Greek style. The proponents of the *gusto Greco* claimed that Greece was "the Place where the most beautiful Edifices were erected, and where the purest and most elegant Examples of ancient Architecture are to be discovered." Furthermore, "as Greece was the great mistress of the arts, and Rome, in this respect, no more than her disciple, it may by presumed, all the most admired building which adorned that imperial city were but imitations of Greek originals."

While many lauded Greek architecture as a more authentic and superior model to emulate, ancient Greek buildings proved too austere to imitate faithfully. When Athenian Stuart designed Spencer House, a London house for the Earl of Spencer, from 1756 to 1766, in an authentically Greek way, Adam, who deferred to Stuart's expertise on Grecian design, marveled on the ceiling decoration and exclaimed they were "Greek to the teeth . . . but by God they are not handsome."

Instead, the delicate linear painting found on Grecian vases emerged as the guiding inspiration of the new Neoclassicism and was applied as decoration on all surfaces of an interior. These vases were commonly referred to as "Etruscan," as they

FACING PAGE

The Painted Room at Spencer House, London, was designed by James "Athenian" Stuart in 1759. Painted grotesque decoration is used on the walls, and ancient stone sources provided inspiration for the furniture. The seat furniture pictured is on loan from the Victoria and Albert Museum, London. © *Spencer House*

LEFT

A panel from the Loggia in the Vatican Palace, Rome, executed under the supervision of Raphael and completed in 1519. The Renaissance interpretation of the ancient grotesque as seen here was taken as a model by Robert Adam and his contemporaries.

LEFT

The Etruscan Dressing Room designed by Robert Adam at Osterley Park was inspired by Sir William Hamilton's vase collection.

This "Etruscan" or Grecian vase was in Sir William Hamilton's famous collection of antiquities and sold to the British Museum in 1772. At the time, it was believed that the decoration depicted the Apotheosis of Homer.

had been mistakenly dubbed in the seventeenth and early eighteenth century. The magnificent collection of vases belonging to Sir William Hamilton, the British envoy to the court of Naples, was published in an illustrated multivolume set in 1766–67 and spurred a mania for vases. A need to own one, or at least a replica, was urgently felt, and urns and vases flooded the market. A prominent luxury manufacturer of the day, Matthew Boulton, capitalized on *le gout grec*. In a letter to bluestocking and society maven Elizabeth Montague, he remarked: "Fashion hath much to do in these things, and as that of the present age distinguishes itself by adopting the most elegant ornaments of the most refined Grecian artists. I am satisfied in conforming thereto, and humbly copying their style, and making new combinations of old ornaments without presuming to invent new ones."

A color palette of terra-cotta, black, ochre, and white was inspired by the vases and was used by Josiah Wedgwood, to whom Sir William Hamilton attributed the dissemination of "a purer taste of forms and ornament," for his different lines of ceramics, many in urn and vase shapes, produced in his factory named Etruria. Adam adapted this color scheme to dramatic effect in the dressing room of the Countess of Derby at Osterley Place. In *Works* Adam directly credited the ancient vases for his inspiration at Osterley: "A mode of Decoration . . . which differs from anything hitherto practiced in Europe . . . imitated from the vases and urns of the Etruscans."

Although "Etruscan" vases undoubtedly turned Adam's head along with the rest of the bon ton, it was the wall decoration, based on ancient Greek and Roman grotesque murals, by such Renaissance masters as Raphael and Giulio Romano at the Loggia in the Vatican and the villas Madama and Pamphili in the 1520s, that formed the basis of quintessential Adam decoration. Adam and his contemporaries believed that these Italian Renaissance interpretations were the best models for how classical wall paintings looked when first completed.

This grotesque wall decoration consisted of medallions and rectangular panels interconnected with scrollwork and classical motifs, and its application in paint was taken as a defining feature. A preference for flat decoration ensued and exuberantly carved three-dimensional Rococo extravagancies were replaced by painted, inlaid, or low-relief ornamentation. Adam pronounced in *Works* that a sense of movement was vitally important and created "an agreeable and diversified contour, that groups and contours like a picture, and creates a variety of light and shade, which gives great spirit, beauty and affect to the composition." Grotesque decoration, of course, successfully kept the eye dancing.

THE ADAM INTERIOR

At the end of the seventeenth century, only royalty and a select few among the nobility put any thought into the design of a room, but, by Adam's time, any family with disposable income and pretensions to polite society made an effort. The top strata of society hired an architect who chose colors, furniture, fabric, etc. Indeed, it was the choice of *which* architect to use that made a statement about their taste.

The merchant-and-professional class were motivated by comfort and conveying their prosperity. More households than ever had fully outfitted rooms that were organized around specific activities. Attention and money were lavished on achieving this. A Frenchman touring in Britain was astounded by the extent of this: "It is indeed remarkable that the English are so much given to the use of mahogany; not only are their tables generally made of it, but also their doors and seats and handrails

Mrs. Congreve and Her Daughters in Their London Drawing Room by Philip Reinagle, 1782, gives a more realistic impression of how most genteel drawing rooms looked. Oval mirrors and a fold-over side table update the room that retains a set of slightly outmoded mahogany dining chairs.

of their staircases. Yet it is just as dear in England as it is in France." Many visitors commented on the comfort and tidiness of English interiors, drawing a portrait of a house-proud nation.

One of the most interesting characteristics of British urban living is that the layout of their dwellings was arranged vertically, not horizontally like the French and most of the Continent. Confined by narrow plots, town houses were built ever upward. The upper strata of society, of course, had their large country estates, but owned or let a town house during the London season, set by when Parliament was in session, which was anytime after Christmas until mid-August, when grouse season began. Those with ample means were able to continue observing the Palladian practice of the *piano nobile*, and maintained drawing rooms on the first floor, and bedrooms above. In more modest homes, the principal reception rooms were near the entrance on the ground floors because of space constraints.

A giltwood oval mirror, circa 1785, with border plates interspersed with patera.

Only the very wealthy could afford to hire Adam as their architect, because nothing in his integrated interiors was ready-made. Door jambs, escutcheons, window hinges all received the attention of Adam's eagle eye. The execution was just as important, and, if need be, he would import Italian craftsmen to create the stucco ceiling decoration exactly how he had seen it in Italy. (As evidence of how ensconced Adam was in the highest echelons of society, almost all his pallbearers at his funeral in 1792 were former clients, and every one of them was a member of the aristocracy.)

To keep things lively and varied, Adam preferred succeeding rooms to be of different shapes and sizes. This was a natural progression in interior planning under the influence of the Picturesque movement, which valued informality and the endless variety of nature. Adam took great pains with his floor plans, which he considered "essential, both to the splendor and convenience of life." He explains at length his plans for Syon House, a commission from the Duke of Northumberland who was known for his educated taste as well as his great wealth:

FOLLOWING PAGES
A longitudinal section of a town mansion from 1774 by John Yenn is invaluable for its depiction of the disbursement of rooms as well as interior decoration. The first floor shows the most amount of embellishment and up-to-date fashions for the drawing room and state bedchamber, which was appropriate. The dining room below is more conservative and restrained.

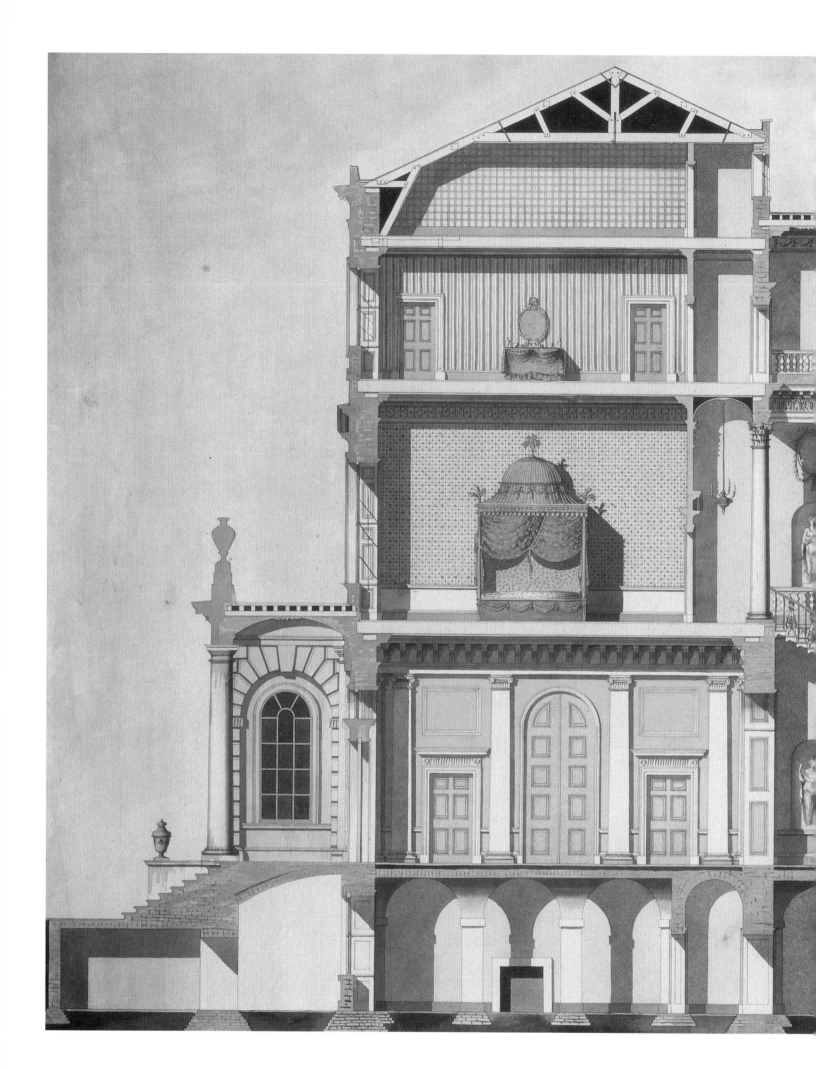

The hall, both in our houses, and in those of France, is a spacious apartment, intended as a room of access where servants in livery attend. It is here a room of great dimension, is finished with stucco, as halls always are, and is formed with a recess at each end, one square and the other circular, which have a noble effect and increases the variety . . . The anti-rooms on each side, are for the attendance of servants out of livery, and also for that of tradesmen. . . . [Adjacent are] the public and private eating-rooms. . . . Next to the great eating-room, lies a splendid with-drawing room, for the ladies, or *salle de compagnie*, as it is called in French. It gives access into a gallery of great length, and is finished in a style to afford great variety and amusement; and is, for this reason, an admirable room for the reception of company after dinner, or for the ladies to retire to after it: For the with-drawing room lying between this and the eating-room, prevents the noise of men being troublesome. [At each end is a closet] the one circular for china, and the other square for miniatures. . . . The great circular saloon serves also for a room of general rendezvous, and for public entertainments. . . .

The duchess's private apartments, he continued, comprised her "bed-chamber, an anti-room for the attendance of her maids, her toilet or dressing-room, her powdering-room, water-closet," with corresponding rooms for the duke, excepting another bedchamber. (This indicated that the duke and duchess shared a bedchamber, a practice that differed from a comparable couple in France.)

Adam's comments on dining rooms are particularly enlightening. He declared that English dining rooms demanded more attention, as opposed to those in France, because:

Accustomed by habit, or induced by the nature of our climate, we indulge more largely in the enjoyment of the bottle . . . The eating rooms are considered as the apartments of conversation, in which we are to pass a great part of our time. This renders it desireable to have them fitted with elegance and splendor, but in a style different from that of the other apartments. Instead of being hung with damask, tapestry, &c they are always finished with stucco, and adorned with statues and paintings, that they may not retain the smell of victuals. . . . Soon after dinner the ladies retire. . . . Left alone, they [the men] resume their seats, evidently more at ease, and the conversation takes a different turn—less reserved—and either graver, or more licentious.

The importance he placed on the social rituals of the dining room resulted in his invention of the sideboard. Long after-dinner conversations necessitated a chamberpot being stowed somewhere in the dining room, and, as a result, many sideboards often have a discreet door on the side.

Painted decoration was the ultimate way to treat the interior in a palette of "light greens, soft blues, weak whites, pink reds, and violets" in addition to the "Etruscan" terra-cotta and black. These rich colors contrasted dramatically to the muted stone, straw, and pea-green shades that were widely available. The ornate walls, now enlivened with grotesque ornament, prompted the simplification of architectural fittings. As the ceiling became the room's focal point, the chimney

The Great Hall at Syon House was designed by Robert Adam for the Duke of Northumberland who was noted for his discerning taste.

This 1762 design by Robert Adam for the west end of the dining room at Kedleston Hall shows a sideboard with pedestals set back in a recessed niche, a favorite Adam device.

receded. Adam often began with the design of the ceiling with the carpet and everything else following. Panels were painted first on canvas or paper which was then affixed to the ceiling. Composition, papier-mâché, or other molded substances were often used to create the illusion of low-relief carving. For those without an architect, ornament was available ready-made. Wallpaper resembling chintz, murals, Gothic tracery, and stucco ornament was available for purchase.

Divided and festoon (or pull-up) curtains were both used, with divided becoming the most fashionable by 1780. On these "French draw" or "French rod" curtains, pelmets were optional, and rods and rings made to be shown were now available. An interior muslin curtain or roll-up blind was hung to diffuse the light and protect the valuable furniture, fabrics, and paintings from fading. Light materials, such as silks, chintzes, and calicoes, were favored for easy operation. Seat and bed upholstery was en suite with walls and curtains. The new informality led to slipcovers being used all the time, and they even appeared in portraits.

By now British-made fitted carpeting was used widely in better homes. Brussels carpeting with a looped pile now joined the available possibilities and was manufactured by the Kidderminster factories. Like Wilton carpets, although less

expensive, they were made in strips of up to three feet in width and woven in small scale repeating patterns conducive to covering variously sized rooms. The carpets Adam designed were individual creations that reflected a particular room's scheme and were derived from the ceiling. Knotted, not looped, carpets made at the Axminster and Moorfields factories were able to recreate his complicated and varying designs.

It had been the custom when entertaining to arrange a circle of chairs for the female guests with the hostess taking pride of place in an armchair next to the warmth of the fireplace. If gentlemen were present, they stood in the center of the circle conversing with each other. The mood for such organized interplay shifted and the break up of the circle was a visible sign of the age's penchant for informality. The celebrated novelist and diarist Fanny Burney noted in 1782 that a hostess exclaimed, "My whole care is to prevent a circle." She then "pulled about the chairs and planted the people in groups with as dexterous disorder as you would desire to see." However, even elaborately painted and papered rooms still had chair rails, simulated or real, so chairs and settees were dragged backed to the wall as soon as the guests left.

Attributed to Henry Walton (British, 1746–1813), A Gentleman at Breakfast, c. 1775–80. Oil on canvas. Toledo Museum of Art; Gift of an anonymous donor, 1956.77. Checked protective slipcovers are kept on the set of chairs.

An assortment of publications providing recommendations on different aspects of interior design was newly and readily available. Clients had an enormous array of options and could take more control of the furnishing of their homes. Their choices also transformed their interiors as personal expressions of taste. The practice for architects to design the *meublant*—the furniture around a room that wouldn't be moved, such as pier tables and mirrors—left the cabinetmaker or upholsterer to supply the *courant*, such as chairs, fire screens, card tables, etc. Adam worked with the workshops of Thomas Chippendale, Ince and Mayhew, and John Linnell to manufacture his designs. For the many items that an architect didn't design, these workshops were trusted by their very particular clients to design and manufacture sophisticated furniture.

Fashionable, well-made furniture was readily available to the middle class who continued to play an important role in the consumer market. As England's trading connections and manufacturing capabilities expanded, it gained an international reputation for goods more sensible than high-style. In the 1786 *Journal des Luxus und der Moden* remarked that "English furniture is almost without exception solid and practical; French furniture is less solid, more contrived, and more ostentatious."

A mahogany window seat designed by Robert Adam in 1764 for the gallery at Croome Court was acquired for another Adam residence, Kenwood House, where it is now on view. Its tapering legs displaced the Rococo's cabriole legs and were the new silhouette of the period.

FACING PAGE
A 1778 engraving of a recently excavated ancient Roman vase on tripod published in Vasi, Candelabri, Cippi, Sarcofagi *by Giovanni Battista Piranesi, whose drawing style Adam studied and imitated.*

This satinwood demi-lune commode is a documented Thomas Chippendale piece made for Denton Hall in 1778 and is now in the collection of the Carnegie Museum. The decoration and shape of the commode make this an example of Chippendale's later work in the Neoclassical style not seen in the celebrated Director.

The oval, or "wheel," back of this mahogany side chair, circa 1780, is centered with a favored Robert Adam motif, the sunflower, an emblem of Apollo, god of music and the arts.

Furniture

The light and elegant ornaments imitated from the ancient works in the Baths and Villas of the Romans, were soon applied in design for chairs, tables, carpets and every other species of furniture.

—ROBERT ADAM

The heavy carving and whiplash curves of English Rococo furniture had no place in Adam's interiors. Instead, he channeled the spirit of the ancients and applied his graceful husk garlands and urns to lighter and more severe furniture forms. "The lightest and most beautiful of [Greek and Roman furniture] are almost universally distinguished by straight or angular lines." Lightness in the design of all things, including furniture, was exceedingly important to Adam. "All . . . furniture is Beautiful in proportion to the smallness of its quantity of Matter, or the Fineness and Delicacy of the Parts of it. Strong and Massy Furniture is everywhere vulgar and unpleasing."

The lines of Louis XVI furniture heavily influenced the desire for more recti-linear shapes, and fauteuils, bergeres, and commodes were all called by their French names. The curvaceous cabriole leg became attenuated and ultimately discarded for the square tapering leg. Classical ornament, such as the sunflower, an emblem of Apollo, and the anthemion, an ancient Greek palmette motif, was grafted onto these modified shapes. It wasn't until the end of the century, when archaeologically correct classical furniture forms would be adopted wholesale. The first infiltration of classically derived forms was the modeling of pedestals after a bronze sphinx tripod brazier found at Pompeii and a very timid version of the klismos (or sabre) leg as

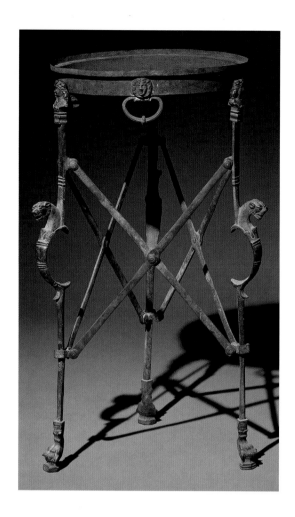

An ancient Roman bronze tripod stand
used in ceremonial rites was found in
the mid-eighteenth-century excavations
at Pompeii and served as a model for
furniture during the Neoclassical period.

RIGHT
This giltwood console table, circa 1770,
is an extremely sophisticated example of
the Neoclassical taste. The rams-headed
monopodia were inspired by ancient
Roman furniture unearthed at Pompeii.

FACING PAGE
Quintessential George Hepplewhite–
style mahogany side chairs nestle up to
a dining table in this room by Dennis
Rolland.

A classical urn enriches the pediment of the cabinet in this living room.

seen in a George Hepplewhite design that was most likely extrapolated from Greek vase decoration.

It is George Hepplewhite's *The Cabinet-Maker and Upholsterer's Guide; or repository of designs for every article of household furniture, in the newest and most approved taste* published in 1788, with the engravings dated 1787, that best illustrates British Neoclassical furniture from the age of Adam. It was brought out after Hepplewhite's death in 1786 by his widow Alice. Like Chippendale's *Director*, these designs were not innovations, but reflected the current furniture fashions. Little is known about Hepplewhite's life, and, unlike Chippendale, he did not have a large London workshop carrying out commissions for important clients. His *Guide* records such new shapes as the shield-back chair and the D-shaped side table. The new ubiquitous use of the oval shape is important to note; it was associated with Greek taste and applied to everything, including mirrors, pembroke tables, and chair backs. Cut in half, it formed a bow or D-shape that was popular for side tables and commodes, which ideally were resting under a mirror whose reflection provided the missing half.

By 1780 oval and shield-back chairs and settees replaced the rectangular interlaced backs illustrated at length in Chippendale's *Director*. The Prince of Wales plume decoration, consisting of three feathers and derived from the prince's crest, was a popular embellishment for chair backs. The lyre-back, a more unusual form, was first devised by Adam for Sir Rowland Winn at Nostell Priory in 1768. The lyre recalled Apollo, patron of music and the arts. Seats were at an all-time width to accommodate hoopskirts and women who "occupied the space of six men." Most often, seat furniture was covered in cotton and linens to match the wall hangings (or wallpaper) and curtains. Leather and horsehair were recommended for dining-room chairs, while silk, brocade, and French tapestry (the most extravagant) were used in houses of the rich. Any drawing room with pretensions was furnished with one or a pair of sofas, and, according to Hepplewhite, "an elegant drawing-room with modern furniture, was scarcely complete without a *confidante*." The ends of the *confidante* were in the form of bergere chairs that pulled up to the ends of a sofa. As before, the seat furniture, designed en suite, was lined up against the dado (chair) rail on the wall when not in use.

Adam and his contemporaries took great pains to design the friezes of pier and side tables to coordinate with the dado so that they appeared as extensions of the wall. The tops of side tables were made to overhang the back so they could sit above the rail—when the back of the top is flush with the table's frieze, the table's top has most likely been cut down at one time. The primary function of the pier and side table was to convey elegance, not utility, making them ideal candidates for delicate painted or gilt decoration. Wired swags made of composition, a mixture of whiting, resin, and size (a glue-like substance), were sometimes applied to form an apron.

A design for side chairs illustrating the fashionable oval and shield-back chairs was included in George Hepplewhite's 1788 first edition of The Cabinet-Maker and Upholsterer's Guide, *but omitted from the 1794 third edition.*

Composition and wire help create delicate pendant floral roundels on this pair of exquisite giltwood marble-top side tables, circa 1775.

The frieze on this demi-lune giltwood and satinwood side table, circa 1775, is elaborately worked with floral roundels to coordinate with the room's dado rail.

FACING PAGE

A sophisticated example of the Neoclassical style, this marquetry demi-lune commode, circa 1775, from a Robert Adam design, is embellished with classical griffins, vases, and garlands. A variety of woods are used, including sycamore stained dark brown and green, for a rich, polychrome appearance.

RIGHT & FACING PAGE
The lyre, an ancient musical instrument associated with Apollo, was first incorporated into a chair back, as seen on these beautifully carved mahogany chairs, circa 1770, by Robert Adam.

Tables of all kinds sat atop tapering legs—usually square but sometimes round, and occasionally enriched with reeding and channeling carved in low relief or bellflower garland inlays. The spade foot was the most common termination.

Commodes were used interchangeably with or in addition to pier and side tables in the drawing room. "Being used in principle rooms, [they] require considerable elegance," and provided the benefit of storage space. Marble, preferred in France for the tops of tables and commodes, was eschewed for painted and inlaid tops. Fine gilt-metal mounts imported from France started appearing on furniture, primarily the side table and commode. Most often applied to the feet and corners, they offered protection as well as an agreeably French accent.

Large mirrors were essential for an impressive drawing room. Plates over sixty-six inches in height were imported, and with the addition of custom duties were only within the realm of the super-rich. Adam favored oval-shaped mirrors with elaborate teetering crestings that defied gravity with the use of composition and wire. Girandoles were also employed liberally and were ideal for Adam's confectionary treatment. Picture and mirror frames were almost always gilt. Water gilding was the costliest and most desirable method as it could be burnished to a high gleam.

The most enduring furniture innovation during the Neoclassical period was the introduction of the sideboard by Adam. With a pair of knife boxes on top, the sideboard was accompanied by a pair of pedestals surmounted by urns that served as cisterns for water to rinse drinking glasses. The pedestal was a cupboard that oftentimes was lined with lead to be used as a basin, while the other pedestal might be used as a plate warmer. Adam liked to design recessed niches, based on the ancient Roman baths, in which to place his sideboards. By the time Hepplewhite's *Guide* was published, sideboards with deep drawers that eliminated the need for the pedestals were equally fashionable.

The Pantheon Macaroni: The epitome of vanity was the macaroni, or dandy, who in the 1770s was a fashionable gentleman who had adopted, as a result of his travels to France and Italy, an ostentatious and flamboyant style of Continental dress, and often, as seen here, a towering hairstyle.

The hinged top of this mahogany dressing table with dramatic laburnum banding opens to a ratcheted mirror and lidded compartments to house all the necessaries for one's toilette.

This rare satinwood and inlaid table, circa 1790, formerly in the Untermeyer Collection at the Metropolitan Museum of Art, serves as both a writing and dressing table, with a hinged top that opens to a ratcheted mirror and a pull-out writing slide. Its Continental shape and sophisticated marquetry give it an attribution to the Swedish émigré cabinetmaker Christopher Furlogh.

The silk-lined screen slides up on this beautifully inlaid maple ladies' work table, circa 1780, which was designed to protect its owner from the heat of the fire and keep her cheek from turning an unbecoming red.

FACING PAGE
In the eighteenth century, sideboards were groaning with prized silver and porcelain; Ellie Cullman of Cullman and Kravis displays a collection of cut-glass on hers. Instead of a cellaret underneath, Cullman strikes an informal note and places a copper basin brimming with pine cones.

ABOVE
Knife boxes, like this delightfully inlaid satinwood pair, circa 1790, were placed on top of sideboards.

BELOW
Pedestals, such as this mahogany pair, generally flanked sideboards. Urn-shaped wine coolers with gilt-metal handles and spigots sit on top.

Cellarets, like this oval one, circa 1780, were lined with aluminum so that they could be filled with ice for chilling wine and were stowed underneath the sideboard when not in use.

179

Ancient Roman tripod incense burners found at Pompeii inspired the form of the pair of giltwood torchères by the window in this dining room by Dennis Rolland.

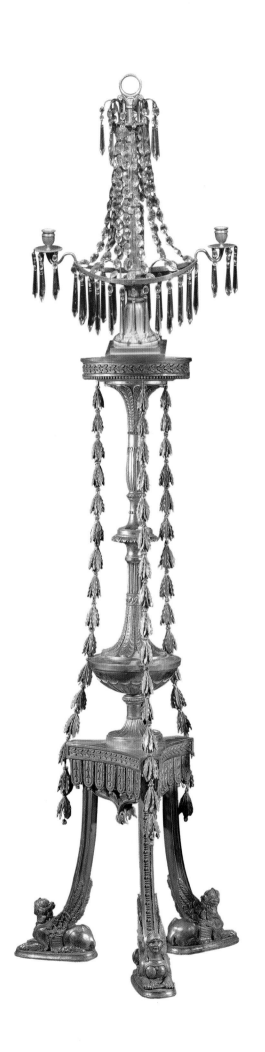

Finely carved sphinxes threaten to fly away with these giltwood torchères, circa 1775, fulsomely enriched with urns, laurel leaves, and husk garlands.

Gilt furniture coordinated beautifully with the painted interiors of the Age of Adam. This pair of armchairs in the manner of John Linnell, circa 1770, is finely molded with Neoclassical detailing such as bellflower garlands and fluting; the wide seats also allowed for the fashionable wide hoopskirts of the day.

The classic library armchair is updated with square tapering legs on this pair of mahogany armchairs, circa 1775.

Pedestals in general regained favor for holding vases, candelabra, and busts in halls, staircases, and galleries. The tripod form based on ancient Roman examples was especially popular and used by Athenian Stuart, Adam, and others.

The neat lines of the secretary were as desirable if not more so than the traditional bureau bookcase. Instead of a slanted fall front that is supported on lopers, "the accommodations for writing are produced by the face of the upper drawer falling down by means of a spring and quadrant, which produces the same usefulness as the flap to a desk." Breakfront bookcases were also often designed with a secretary drawer. Hepplewhite gave his secretaries, as well as his chests of drawers and commodes, the option of traditional bracket feet or the more fashionable outswept splayed feet.

The dressing table was lavished with attention during this period. This was the age of the macaroni, of towering hairstyles that reached outlandish heights abetted by wire, and when extravagant amounts of time and money were spent on appearances. Even Wedgwood capitalized on the rampant vanity and manufactured dentures out of costly porcelain. A lady's dressing table contained compartments for "combs, powders, essences, pin-cushions, and other necessary equipage." A ratcheted mirror was designed to eliminate the need for a separate standing mirror. Sumptuous materials, such as expensive satinwood and intricate inlay, were appropriate for this item whose beauty reflected its owner's.

No drawing room was complete without a sofa, like this mahogany example, circa 1775.

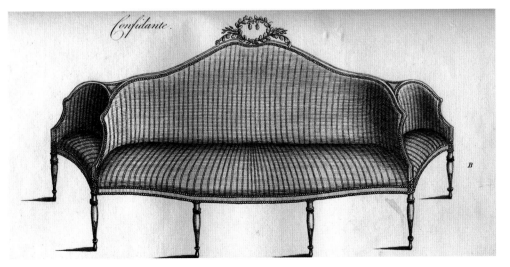

This design for a confidante was "of French origin, and is in pretty general request for large and spacious suites of apartments," according to George Hepplewhite.

The design of the curious turtle-and-shell marquetry (detail) on this hare-wood and marquetry commode, circa 1780, are related to those published in the 1785 The Ladies' Amusement, or Whole Art of Japanning Made Easy *by Robert Sayer, which were copied extensively by silversmiths, japanners, and textile designers.*

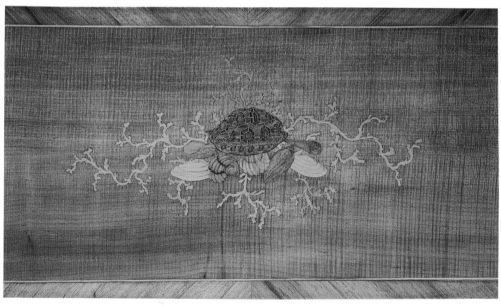

Restrained inlay and beautiful cuts of mahogany embellish this serpentine commode, circa 1785.

The serpentine lines of the Rococo are gently modified on this mahogany and satinwood commode (from a pair) attributed to John Cobb, circa 1770.

Adam loved the oval shape, which was revered by the Greeks as perfect, and applied it frequently to mirrors, as on this giltwood mirror, circa 1775.

A design from Robert and James Adam's 1773 Works in Architecture.

From a Robert Adam design, this imposing mirror, circa 1775, reaches to nearly nine feet with an elaborate urn and garland cresting.

Girandoles, such as this elaborate gilt-wood pair, circa 1775, were ideal for Adam's intricate confectionary treatment of ornament.

The last major change that radically effected how furniture looked was the predilection for flat decoration. Painted furniture was the preferable way to coordinate with the wall and ceiling decoration of an Adam interior. Gilt furniture was also considered sympathetic to a painted interior. The carcass, made of a soft, inexpensive wood, such as beech, was primed and painted. The Swiss artist Angelica Kauffman's highly detailed paintings of classical scenes were extremely influential and widely imitated. When incorporated into ceilings and furniture, her scenes were contained within rectangular panels and integrated into Adam's characteristic delicate grotesque of urns, paterae, and flower garlands. She is recorded as having been in the employ of Adam beginning in 1771, several years after emigrating to Britain in 1766. Kauffman worked on the decoration of Syon, Saltram, and Home House, among others, and was married at one time to the painter Antonio Zucchi, who also worked on many Adam projects.

While painted furniture was popular, inlaying "light and elegant ornaments" was more common and practical than painting them onto furniture, and it gradually superceded carving as the main decorative technique of the period. The predilection for colored decoration resulted in using dramatic contrasting timbers for inlay, and even painting the inlaid wood in the typical Adam colors of blues, greens, pinks, and lilacs.

ABOVE

The superstructure on an intricately inlaid sideboard denotes a Scottish origin.

LEFT

The Neoclassical style's characteristic square tapering legs ending in spade-feet supports are used on this elegant mahogany and satinwood-inlaid sideboard, circa 1780, complete with a drawer fitted for chilling wine.

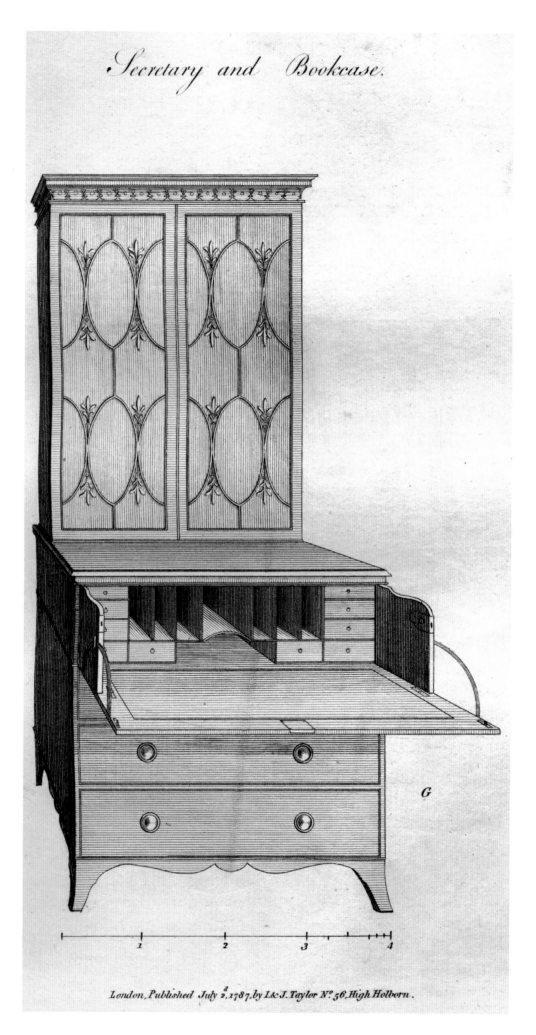

Secretary and Bookcase.

This George Hepplewhite design showcases the new secretaire drawer that
changed the profile of bureau bookcases
to a straight front, moving away from
the traditional slanted fall front.

FACING PAGE
What looks like a commode is actually
a bureau on this magnificent satinwood
secretaire cabinet, circa 1780, cleverly
disguised by the newly invented flat-
front secretaire drawer.

G

London, Published July 2, 1787, by I. & J. Taylor N⁰ 56, High Holborn.

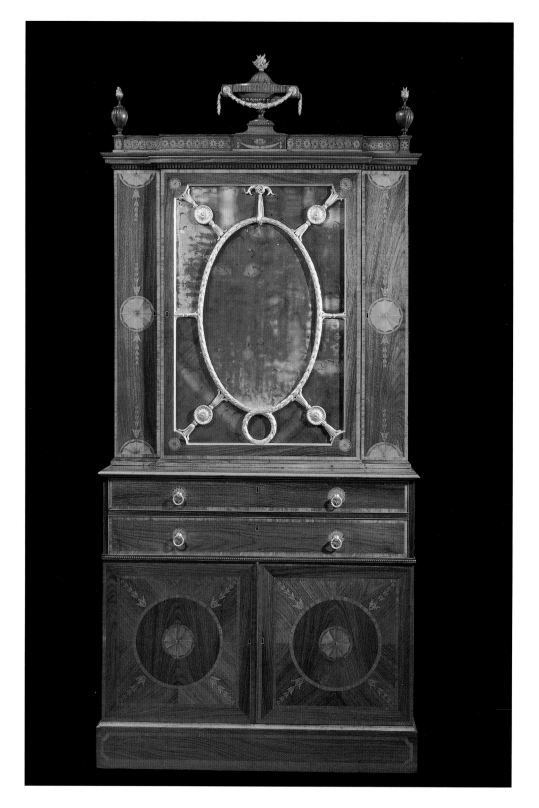

An important rosewood secretaire book-case, attributed to Thomas Chippendale, circa 1775.

The oval fan patera, inspired by the shape of ancient Greek and Roman ceremonial saucers, was a motif that was exceptionally popular. Hot sand was often employed to singe and shade the edges for a richer effect. The firm of Ince and Mayhew were particularly known for their exquisitely inlaid furniture. A variety of exotic timbers, shading, staining, and surface engraving were employed to create sophisticated pieces that rivaled painted decoration in its intricacy. Other workshops also specialized in inlay, and ready-made marquetry panels were available for purchase.

Mahogany remained a staple for dining room and library furniture, but it was the golden satinwood that was brought into the drawing room. The earliest and, by many accounts, the most beautiful variety was imported from the West Indies (and more specifically Puerto Rico). Its figure is similar to plum-pudding mahogany, with rippled waves. Satinwood from Ceylon was also imported, but generally considered inferior, as most logs had a plain figure. The expense and hardness of satinwood made it a poor candidate for carving, and it was used mainly as a veneer.

RIGHT & BELOW
Painted panels depicting scenes from the life of Odysseus's wife Penelope are after the work of Angelica Kauffman. This side table, originally from a pair, was most likely designed by Robert Adam for the second withdrawing room at 20 St. James

FACING PAGE
The second withdrawing room at 20 St. James Square retains the original ceiling decoration designed by Robert Adam.

Pl. 66.

Tops for　Pier Tables, &c.

London, Published July 2ᵈ, 1787, by I. & J. Taylor, Nº 56, High Holborn.

FACING PAGE
George Hepplewhite offers a variety of shapes and decoration for pier tables in this design.

ABOVE RIGHT
A very important bedroom must have been the home of this richly inlaid satinwood bedside cupboard, circa 1790.

ABOVE
This exquisite cream-painted and gilt pembroke table, circa 1770, was part of a suite of painted furniture, including a settee, chairs, and firescreen, belonging to James Bonnell at Upton Place, Essex.

RIGHT
The attenuated cabriole legs of this mahogany and satinwood-inlaid side table, attributed to John Cobb, circa 1780, are modified from the Rococo's more full-bodied version and were regarded as being very French in style.

The low-relief carving of berried foliage and shamrocks on this mahogany table, circa 1765, is exceptionally Irish.

This harewood and parquetry commode, circa 1775, is executed in the French taste with its bombé shape, overall inlaid decoration, and gilt-metal sabot mounts. It is attributed to Pierre Langlois, a French émigré cabinetmaker working in London in the mid-eighteenth century who supplied items executed in the latest Parisian styles.

The large inlaid oval paterae on the doors of this satinwood
commode, which were an immensely popular embellishment on
Neoclassical furniture, are derived from ancient ceremonial saucers.

RIGHT

This pair of intricately inlaid satinwood demi-lune side tables, circa 1775, is attributed to John Mayhew and William Ince, who produced some of the finest examples of marquetry furniture in the Neoclassical taste. The firm's collaboration with the architects Robert Adam and Sir William Chambers undoubtedly influenced their repertoire of classical motifs and graceful forms.

William Moore of Dublin, who worked for Ince and Mayhew before opening his own workshop in Ireland, is most likely the maker of this beautifully inlaid satinwood pembroke table, circa 1780.

ભ   ભ   ભ

FACING PAGE

Unusual musical trophies are inlaid into a beautifully figured satinwood cabinet in this sitting room by Nancy Serafini of Homeworks.

FOLLOWING PAGES

Satinwood can be difficult to integrate with other woods, but Cullman and Kravis, by painting the walls a rich goldenrod, expertly pair mahogany and satinwood in this opulent dining room.

At long last, a homegrown style was conceived that paid homage to the country's reverence for antiquity *and* satisfied its insatiable appetite for variety. Suspicious of the exuberance of the Rococo, an audience awaited and enthusiastically received Robert Adam's ebullient version of Neoclassicism. His attendance to all parts of an interior coincided with the influx of fashion-related publications that advised on how best to appoint a gracious home resulting in a revolution in the conception of a room as a complete and distinctive space.

However, fashion and those that direct it are fickle, and the endless quest for something new, led by the Prince of Wales, soon left many dissatisfied with Adam's "gingerbread and sippets of embroidery." It would no longer be enough to imitate the ornaments on ancient baths and villas; instead, the stone and bronze furniture that ancients sat on would be forged in mahogany and rosewood and displayed in the drawing rooms and libraries of Britain.

THE REGENCY

LUXURY AND COMFORT
1790–1830

I do not believe that, since the days of Heliogabalus, there has been such magnificence and such luxury.

—PRINCESS LIEVEN on Carlton House

To many, the Regency period is the most glamorous period in British design, with precision of detail, purity of line, and richness of materials producing some of the most high-style decorative arts in history. Although the true "Regency" period technically spans 1811 through 1820, when the Prince of Wales served as regent during the illness of his father, George III, it culturally refers to the time from when the prince's influence on taste was first felt until the end of his reign as George IV, in 1830. During these four decades, he emerged as the first royal arbiter of taste since William III, and his whims in fashion were so compelling that even a tour he made of Scotland in 1823 would precipitate a craze for tartans and all things Scottish.

Although his legacy as a patron of the arts is incomparable, the prince's financial excesses made him one of the most disliked British sovereigns on record. He was such a voracious spender that by the time he became regent, he was already over £500,000 in debt. Even so, his desire for constant improvements and changes to his palaces could not be curbed, and no sooner was a refurbishment completed than he began again. Moral philosophers preached against lavishness and its consequent lapse of character, with the prince held up as the prime example. The architect Robert Smirke counseled, "As the moral character is corrupted by luxury, so is art vitiated by the exuberance of its ornaments. . . . An excess of ornament is . . . the symptom of a vulgar and degenerate taste."

Two main phases emerge during the Regency: its beginnings are marked by the transition of design from the profuse ornamentation and attenuated proportions of Robert Adam to the clean, crisp lines characteristic of the French Directoire style. In the later, full-blown Regency, a new understanding of the antique style took hold, resulting in a desire to replicate the furniture of the ancients closely, instead of

ABOVE
The clean lines and graphic juxta-position of giltwood and rosewood on an early Regency side table blend seamlessly in this contemporary room by Bruce Norman Long.

RIGHT
This iconic painting of Madame Recamier shows her reclining on a Grecian couch, an immensely popular form of seat furniture in the early nine-teenth century. Her house, decorated in the latest style by Percier and Fontaine, was an essential stop for visitors in Paris.

merely applying classical ornament to European forms. Ladies now donned Grecian chemises while reclining on Grecian couches.

Concurrent with the classical mood of austere sobriety, was the continuing appeal of the picturesque and the value on informality and comfort. A collective unbuttoning of the stays resulted in more casual etiquette, dress, and interiors. To the surprise of foreigners, the English pulled their sofas and chairs around the fireplace and *left* them there.

EARLY REGENCY STYLE

Upon reaching his majority, the Prince of Wales was given Carlton House off of Pall Mall, the former residence of his deceased grandmother Augusta, the dowager Princess of Wales. Its refurbishment undertaken between 1783 and 1787 was a collaboration with the architect Henry Holland and a team of Anglo-French craftsmen and was the first important project in which the prince was able to give free reign to his love for interior design. The results, which were more closely allied to the French Directoire style of severe classicism, were copied enthusiastically by the bon ton. Horace Walpole wrote the Countess of Upper Ossory, "We went to see the Prince's new palace in Pall Mall and were charmed. It will be the most perfect in Europe. There is an August simplicity that astonished me. You cannot call it magnificent; it is the taste and propriety that strike." The prince characteristically redecorated Carlton House once more before it was demolished in 1827. By this time he had moved on to transforming Buckingham House into Buckingham Palace, the new chief royal residence, and additional building programs at Windsor Castle and the Brighton Pavilion.

A view of the Chinese Drawing Room at the Prince of Wales's Carlton House published in Thomas Sheraton's Cabinet-Maker and Upholsterer's Drawing-Book *in 1794. A more full-bodied version of chinoiserie would be embraced by the prince in the early nineteenth century at Brighton Pavilion.*

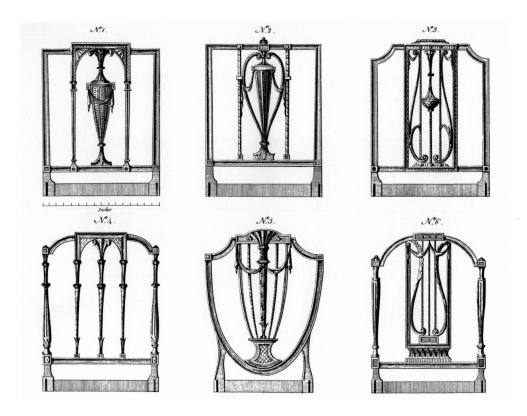

A 1792 design for the backs of parlor chairs (as opposed to the more formal drawing-room chairs) from Thomas Sheraton's seminal Cabinet-Maker and Upholsterer's Drawing-Book.

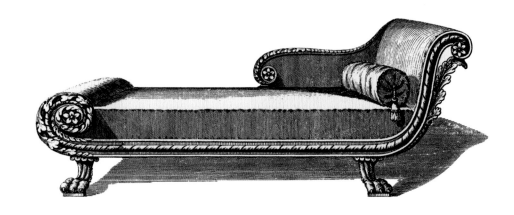

Thomas Sheraton advised that this design of a "Grecian Squab" be executed in "white and gold, or mahogany carved."

As the French Revolution in 1789 set off an influx of émigré craftsmen and wares to Britain's shores, a passion for French fashions swept the upper classes. Sir Gilbert Elliot, a nobleman, observed to his wife in 1790 that "[t]he quantity of French goods of all sorts, particularly ornamental furniture and jewels, has sunk the price of such things here." The dissemination of French fashions continued to exert a powerful influence, especially as the artistry lavished by the French on designs for furnishings and decorative arts was unmatched elsewhere. The furniture designer George Smith lamented, "In France, the first-rate painters do not think themselves degraded by providing Designs for the Cabinet-makers or for the Upholsterer," as, he implies, did English craftsmen artists.

One of the visitors to Carlton House was Thomas Sheraton. Sheraton, in his hugely successful *Cabinet-Maker and Upholsterer's Drawing-Book*, was so taken by the opulent mansion that he included a depiction of the prince's Chinese Drawing Room. Sheraton's book was influential, internationally successful, and besides shaping American taste which continued to be a receptive audience of English fashions, it was copied in Scandinavia, Germany, and Central Europe. First published in installments between 1791 and 1794, it was the most influential and most important pattern book to disseminate taste until the next century.

Although Sheraton's pattern books have made him illustrious to posterity, he lived and died in chronic poverty. His obituary described him as having once been a journeyman cabinetmaker, but supported his family for many years with his drawings. His designs were intended for practical use by the trade, and his subscribers were made up of craftsmen and artists, not the aristocracy. Sheraton depicted furniture influenced by the refined French fashions currently favored by the Prince of Wales. His designs featured severe and balanced rectilinear forms, delicate inlay, occasional sparingly applied slight carving in low relief, painted enrichments, and a great variety of chair backs and legs, which continue to produce a pleasing impression of lightness and grace. Sheraton's *Cabinet Dictionary* from 1803 introduced more signature Regency features—such as the first illustration of the couch, the ultimate piece of Regency furniture combining classical origins with absolute comfort.

LATE REGENCY STYLE

By 1800 an archaeological approach toward the applied arts soon took hold of design. Beginning in France, where it resonated deeply with the success of the Revolution and evoked a passionate reverence for the example of the ancient republics, it was enthusiastically adapted in a simplified form by the English who were always mad for anything Greek or Roman.

One of the first seminal English publications depicting ancient furniture was directly inspired by the prince's insatiable enthusiasm for variety. His architect, Henry

An illustration, in "Etruscan" outline in imitation of Grecian vase paintings, from John Flaxman's 1792 The Odyssey *shows examples of antique furniture, including the klismos chair. Flaxman supplied many classical drawings for Wedgwood ceramics and became the leading sculptor of his day.*

ABOVE

The Egyptian Room at Thomas Hope's house on Duchess Street, London, was designed to showcase his collection of Egyptian antiquities. Appropriate ornament from mummy cases and papyrus scrolls embellish the walls and furniture in a palette of yellow and blue-green "relieved by masses of black and of gold."

FACING PAGE

This important pair of painted and parcel gilt pedestals of Athenienne form, circa 1810, are illustrated in Thomas Hope's Household Furniture and Interior Decoration *and most likely were among Hope's furnishings in his Duchess Street mansion. Hope esteemed highly the artistry and skill of France's designers and craftsmen, and it isn't surprising that he entrusted the manufacture of his furniture, such as these pedestals, to French carvers and bronze-casters instead of English ones.*

Holland, sent Charles Heathcote Tatham to Italy from 1794 to 1797 in search of new ideas, resulting in the publication *Etchings of Ancient Ornamental Architecture Drawn from the Originals in Rome and Other Parts of Italy during the Years 1794, 1795, and 1796.* It included engraved outline drawings after John Flaxman, whose linear drawings from 1794 of the *Odyssey* and *Iliad* were called by Thomas Hope "the finest modern imitations I know of the elegance and beauty of the ancient Greek attire and furniture, armour, and utensils." Among the influential forms and motifs Tatham recorded was the lion monopodium, a lion's leg surmounted by a lion's head used as a support for tables and chairs copied from marble, stone, and bronze originals.

However, the biggest exponent of late-Regency classicism was the banker and collector Thomas Hope, who took it upon himself to reform English taste. That a member of the professional classes was able to guide fashion in such a way that was formerly the exclusive domain of the aristocracy, is testament to the social changes occurring at that time. After extensive travels in the Mediterranean with stops in such remote locations as Greece, Turkey, Asia Minor, Syria, and Egypt, Hope returned to London and decorated his own town house on Duchess Street with archaeologically correct classical and Egyptian furnishings that provided an appropriate showcase for his collection. An armchair was "adorned with chimaera, copied

PREVIOUS PAGES
The opulent Banqueting Hall, with lotus-flower lamps and a massive one-ton chandelier suspended from the mouths of silvered dragons, was designed in 1815 as the centerpiece of the Brighton Pavilion, the prince's seaside pleasure palace in Brighton.

This mahogany and bronze sideboard was designed by Thomas Hope most likely for his country house, the Deepdene, in Surrey. The four winged "philosophers" are probably taken from Roman busts after Greek representations of Socrates or Aristotle.

Hope designed this vase room to display his extensive collection of Grecian vases, many obtained from the famous collection of Sir William Hamilton.

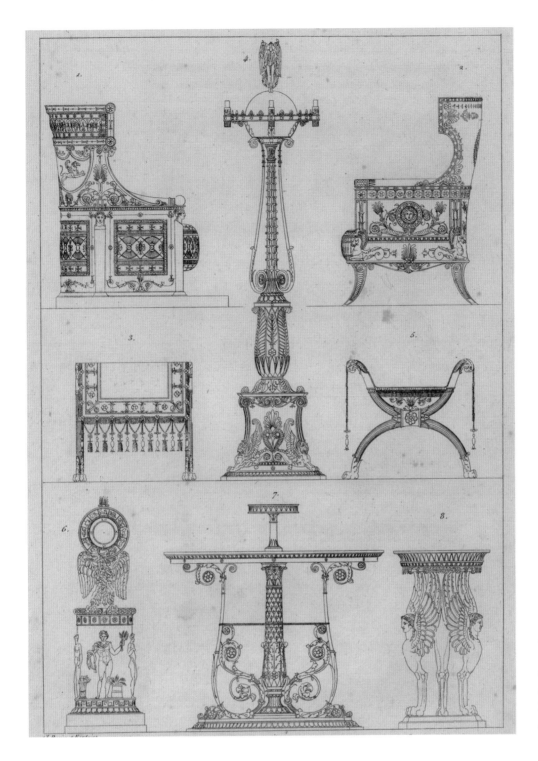

A plate from Percier and Fontaine's 1801 immensely influential Recueil de Decorations interieures comprenant tout ce qui a rapport a l'ameublement, *depicts archaeologically correct furniture forms.*

from a sarcophagus in the collection of Prince Baschi at Rome," and a table with legs similar to "those limbs of ideal animals, adapted to the same purpose which have been found among the remains of Pompeii."

Highlights of Hope's house included three rooms devoted to his collection of vases, including some purchased from Sir William Hamilton, as well as Egyptian- and Indian-themed drawing rooms. In 1807 he published drawings of the house's interiors and furnishings along with his manifesto on taste in *Household Furniture and Interior Decoration* executed from designs, in addition to issuing tickets of admittance for those who wanted to see it. When it came to designing appropriate furniture, he was immensely indebted to the designs of Napoleon's decorators

A 1796 colored lithograph of the Taj Mahal from Thomas and William Daniell's Oriental Scenery, *a multi-volume work with illustrations of India that influenced England's decorative arts.*

Percier and Fontaine and their book *Recueil de Decorations interieures comprenant tout ce qui a rapport a l'ameublement*, which defined France's Empire style. Their designs were so authentic, they said, that they "did not belong to us, it is entirely the property of the ancients." Classical motifs were applied in a symbolic way, and nothing without meaning or purpose was added. A suggestion to embellish a dual-purpose breakfast-and-game table with a "tea tree and coffee plant for its ornaments, with the masks of Ceres and Bacchus . . . perhaps the mask of Comus, the god of festivals and mirth, will be found to accord" demonstrates how rigorously and ridiculously this was adhered to.

George Smith brought Hope's Grecian magnificence to the middle class in his 1808 *Collection of Designs for Household Furniture and Interior Design* so that "the beauty and elegance displayed in the fittings-up of modern houses may not be confined to the stately mansions of our nobility in the metropolis, but be published for the use of the country at large . . ." Although Hope dismissed Smith's designs as "extravagant caricatures," they were instrumental in the reformation of British taste that Hope so desired.

Egyptian ornament was newly introduced into the canon of classically appropriate decoration, bolstered by Napoleon's invasion of Egypt in 1798 and Baron Vivant Denon's 1802 publication *Voyage dans le basse et la haute Egypte*. In England Egyptomania was spurred on by Admiral Nelson's victory defeat of Napoleon on the Nile. His lover, Lady Hamilton, swooningly addressed him as "Duke Nelson, Marquis Nile, Earl Alexandria, Viscount Pyramid, Baron Crocodile, and Prince Victory."

Another style that embellished fashionable interiors was chinoiserie, newly revived by the Prince of Wales. At Carlton House his Chinese Drawing Room piqued the interest of many, but it was the robust cocktail of Chinese, Indian, and Moorish styles at his seaside pleasure palace, the Royal Pavilion, that transformed chinoiserie from a delicate, playful style to a serious one. A nationalist backlash against the pervasive French influence had ensued, and the prince consciously chose a different style. Lady Bessborough confided, "The Prince says he had it so because at that time there was such a cry against French things &c., and he was afraid of his furniture being accus'd of Jacobinism."

Oriental Scenery, the monumental multivolume work by Thomas and William Daniell, featured hand-colored engravings of the topography, architecture, and antiquities of India and immensely influenced the decorative arts. Its exoticism and emphasis on the scenic drew those whose taste veered toward the Romantic, not the classical. Motifs were freely borrowed from Oriental scenery to decorate wallpapers and ceramics, while the flamboyant domes and minarets of the Royal Pavilion at

This extraordinary cabinet (originally from a pair), which incorporates lacquer panels, is characteristic of the Regency's robust chinoiserie.

Brighton were directly inspired by the Daniells' accurate depiction of Indian architecture. Expanded under the auspices of architect John Nash in 1815 with interior decoration overseen by Robert Jones and Frederick Crace, an Oriental extravaganza of serpents, dragons, fretwork, and lotus flowers infused every element.

THE REGENCY INTERIOR

No more the cedar parlour's formal gloom
With dullness chills, 'tis now the living room,
Where guests to whim, to task or fancy true
Scatter'd in groups, their different plans pursue.
Here politicians eagerly relate
The last day's news, or the last night's debate.
Here books of poetry and books of prints
Furnish aspiring artists with new hints . . .
Here, midst exotic plants, the curious maid
Of Greek and Latin seems no more afraid.

—HUMPHRY REPTON

Fragments on the Theory of Landscape Gardening, 1816

A collection of high-style Regency furniture was installed at Sacombe Park, Hertfordshire, including an exotic painted tôle and parcel gilt cabinet, circa 1815, which exemplifies the fusion of Grecian and Oriental made fashionable at Brighton Pavilion.

Even though the cost of living doubled between 1795 and 1820 due to the Napoleonic wars and other factors, it was still observed that "[a]n Englishman delights to show his wealth; every thing in his house, therefore, is expensive." Appointing a fashionable home was easier than ever, and, thanks to industrial advances that put more money in middle-class pockets, more widespread. Numerous shops, smartly decorated with carefully planned glittering displays, attracted large crowds who also flocked to auctions, art exhibitions, and museums of curiosities.

Fashion and style magazines were pervasive with Rudolph Ackermann's *Repository of Arts, Literature, Commerce, Manufactures, Fashion and Politics*, published monthly between 1806 and 1829, serving as one of the best records of the fluctuating fashions for dresses, furniture, and even fabric. With the improvements of communication and transportation facilitated by the new networks of roads and canals, the sophistication of craftsmen and households in provincial cities, such as Liverpool, Manchester, Lancaster, Bath, Birmingham, Bristol, and York, rose exponentially.

If the British looked to others for style inspiration, it was their own comfort and convenience they consulted in arranging their rooms. The natural world held the nation in its thrall, and its untamed wilderness, as romanticized in the poetry of Wordsworth, Keats, and Shelley and the pastoral paintings of Constable and Turner,

encouraged the desire for more informal and unaffected settings. While travel to the Continent was curtailed during the French revolution, the contemporary ardor for the picturesque was fanned by taking in the scenic countryside of the Lake District and Wales.

The most forthright way to get closer to nature was to bring the outdoors inside. The removal of the state apartment, now referred to as the "best bedroom," from the main floor, created space for more common rooms with distinct functions, such as breakfast rooms, billiard rooms, and conservatories. In the great country houses that were built before the Neo-Palladian era of the *piano nobile*, these main rooms were on the ground floor, and with the advent of the double-door "French windows," made possible by glass plates becoming ever larger, one could step directly onto the terrace so as to be "instantly out of doors." However, "the new fashioned windows of Italy opening to the floor" didn't always supply the desired scenic view: "originally intended to survey the lawns, the vistas, and the groves of Claude, in their summer attire, or the canals of Venice are now to be seen in every confounded street of London, that a clear survey may be enjoyed of muddy streets, and to inhale the full fragrance of the effuvia, or dust of scavengers, from below." Even if the view was lackluster, there were plenty of vases of flowers scattered about which for the first time embellished interiors.

The picturesque also saw virtue in the anti-classical asymmetry, as evidenced in the architecture of older houses. Over time, they were invariably enlarged with

A typical drawing from Rudolph Ackermann's Repository of Arts, Literature, Commerce, Manufactures, Fashion and Politics *illustrating the current fashions for the furnishings of a dining room.*

FACING PAGE TOP & BOTTOM *Humphry Repton updates an old-fashioned parlor, with chairs arranged in a circle, to a "Modern Living Room" furnished with books and wall-to-wall carpeting and with access to a conservatory. Note the emphasis on the outdoors and the ability for individuals to pursue separate activities simultaneously.*

wings that affected an irregular, rambling appearance to the house and usually had the virtue of being of a different architectural style. In this way, the eye became accustomed to seeing a profusion of styles living happily together higgledy-piggledy. With houses and rooms no longer symmetrical, it was easy to be seduced into no longer arranging furniture thus.

A requisite of the Romantic life was ownership of an ornamental cottage, a small rustic dwelling where one could easily commune with nature. The architect James Malton advised in *An Essay on Cottage Architecture* that the best style of architecture for such a dwelling was one that replicated "that Peculiar Mode of Building which was originally the Effect of Chance." If Gothic arched windows were used, stained-glass windows were perfect to complete the effect, and oak for "doors, window-frames, floors, skirting, chimney-pieces. Etc., should correspond with the chairs and tables, and be left as from the hands of the carpenter [i.e., not painted]." For its furnishings, an antiquarian approach was thought most suitable. This meant old oak furniture from the early seventeenth century and older that was rarely available in sets and interiors with mismatched furniture of different styles.

The Gothic style, romanticized through its antiquarian associations, gradually became accepted for more than just cottages and emerged as an alternative to the

Large Gothic-arched windows allow one to step "directly out of doors" and provide a picturesque view of landscape from inside.

FACING PAGE
Muted jewel tones and dark furnishings, including a robustly carved pair of rosewood globes, create a relaxing oasis in this gentleman's billiard room by Charlotte Moss.

The south end of St. Michael's Galley at Fonthill Abbey, the extravagant Gothic Revival house of the eccentric and fabulously wealthy William Beckford, completed in 1812. Fonthill's soaring 276-foot-high octagonal tower collapsed dramatically only thirteen years later.

classical for grand buildings. William Beckford's Fonthill Abbey was the most extravagant example designed by James Wyatt. George IV, always part of the vanguard, had Windsor Castle enhanced in the Gothic style by Sir Jeffrey Wyatville, with new suites of state rooms completed in 1828.

No matter if "the house be Grecian or gothic, large or small," wrote Humphrey Repton, the influential landscape architect and writer on the picturesque, the essential rooms "for the present habits of life" were:

> a dining-room and two others, one of which may be called a drawing-room, and the other a book-room, if small, or the library, if large: to these is sometimes added a breakfast room, but of late, especially since the central hall, or vestibule, has been in some degree given up, these rooms have been opened into each other, en suite, by large folding doors; the effect of this enfilade, or visto, through a modern house, is occasionally increased by a conservatory at one end, and repeated by a large mirror at the opposite end.

The Great Library at Cassiobury Park, circa 1815, is furnished comfortably and used equally as a study and sitting room.

FACING PAGE
Layers of rich mahogany add to the studious ambience of this sumptuous library by Ann Getty.

Repton highlights the necessity of a room dedicated to books, and indeed, the country-house library became the center of everyday activities. No longer the domain of the master of the house, it was invaded by the female members of the household who, with the addition of comfortable furnishing, turned it into a relaxed room for company. As described by Maria Edgeworth about her visit to Bowood in 1818:

> the library tho' magnificent is a most comfortable habitable looking room . . . it was very agreeable in the delightful library after breakfast this day—groups round various tables—books and Lady Landsdowne found the battle of Roundway for me in different histories, and Lord Landsdowne showed me a letter of Waller's to Lord Hopton on their quarrey after this battle, and Lord Grenville shaking his leg and reading was silent and I suppose, happy.

The bedchambers, which moved to the upper floors to create room for the library and other common rooms, stayed upstairs. The adjacent dressing rooms were still furnished as sitting rooms, but, away from the rest of the public rooms, were not generally used for visiting.

With the new multiplicity of common rooms, the need for one room to serve several functions was eliminated, and it wasn't long before furniture was left in the

middle of the room, even when not in use. This custom soon made its way to town, and foreigners were shocked by such laxness: "Such is the modern fashion of placing furniture carried to an extreme, as fashions always are, but the apartments of a fashionable house look like an Upholsterer's or Cabinet-maker's Shop."

Innovations in lighting also tremendously changed how people interacted and how furniture was arranged. The illumination of the Argand lamp, patented in 1783 by the Swiss Ami Argand, was exponentially stronger than candlelight; several people were able to cluster together (prompting the need for the center table) and share this one light source. By 1800 it was found in most well-heeled households, although candlelight was still preferred for formal occasions.

The decoration of rooms kept the tradition established by Robert Adam of coordinating each room to an individual theme. At Carlton House, the most important interior of the time, room schemes were based on color or style, such as the Yellow Bow Room, the Blue Bow Room, the disturbingly named Flesh-Coloured Room, the Roman Room, and the Chinese Drawing Room.

The Regency color palette was bolder than ever before, enabled by the expanded variety of available paint colors. The knowledge that the wall paintings of antiquity were originally vibrant and colorful sanctioned such hues. Of all the colors available, red, in shades of crimson, ruby, or maroon, was the quintessential Regency color. "A proper tint of crimson is the richest and most splendid color for the walls of a room." Green, a classic Georgian color, continued to be used throughout, while blue was conventional for bedrooms, and yellow, not commercially available until 1818, controversial. Sir John Soane shocked many with his acid-lemon South Drawing Room in his London home.

A full-blown Greek Revival interior had large areas of plain surfaces with ornament applied sparingly. Walls were painted and papered. Expanses of color were broken up by bold paneled borders, sometimes in papier-mâché low-relief ornament, with the ceiling and moldings handled similarly. Trompe

Crimson, "the richest and most splendid color for the walls of a room," is employed in the dining room at Attingham Park. The plaster decoration applied in bold geometric banding and the wall-to-wall English carpet were de rigueur at the end of the eighteenth century.

l'oeil painted decoration also became fashionable and simulated marble and wood were especially popular. Many have credited the French craftsmen at Carlton House with bringing the skill of faux painting to England. Hand-painted imported Chinese wallpaper was the most expensive and highly desirable, but newly rivaled by French papers. Companies such as Reveillon, Zuber, and Dufour excelled at the artistry of wallpapers and retailed an endless array of patterns, such as panoramic landscapes, trompe l'oeil, stucco ornament, and Gothic tracery.

Fitted carpeting continued to be a staple in the reception rooms of better English homes, complete with a patterned border. Floor cloths were more popular than ever and were advertised as "cool in summer and most useful in winter, because they can be cleaned in long spells of rainy weather by washing them as you would the floor, whereas woolen carpets must remain wet & dirty during bad weather." The renewed interest in chinoiserie caused reed, rush, and straw matting to be reevaluated. No longer only suitable for modest or rustic dwellings, it covered even the floor of the Great Drawing Room in the exalted Carlton House.

This was the era of the upholsterer, and the draping of material and application of trimmings became ever more complicated and theatrical. At the end of the century, festoons of drapery were affixed to *everything*. This fashion was developed and taken to its extreme in France, but spread quickly throughout Europe and the United States. The cost of the acres of fabric used in these interiors was mitigated by advances in transportation and the faster and cheaper output of the new steam-powered cotton mills.

Ruched or festooned pull-up blinds were out of fashion by 1800, with divided curtains supreme. When pelmets

*Satinwood oval panels strikingly
contrast with rich mahogany veneers
on this large bowfront sideboard,
circa 1795.*

were used, they were festoons (of course!) with either short or very long tails, affixed
with bows and rosettes. Sometimes only pelmets were used without curtains, and a
trend for nonfunctioning decorative curtains for windows and niches developed.
"Curtain cornices" in which continuous swags of fabric were draped from pelmet
to pelmet around a room took festooning to the limit. Sub-curtains made out of
muslin, sometimes in combination with blinds, diffused the light, protected fabrics,
and provided some privacy. Heavier textiles and richer colors, usually a shade of
crimson, were warranted in the masculine library and dining room. For "rooms of
a lighter cast" such as the drawing room and bedchamber, lighter fabrics such as
glazed taffeta and tabaray, shortened to "tabby," a half silk of one color often striped
with a satin, were newly acceptable.

The challenge of curtaining pointed Gothic windows was sometimes solved
by using a shaped roller blind painted to resemble stained glass. Painted roller blinds

were widely available and were made out of silk, linen, wire gauze, and paper. Venetian blinds, with the horizontal wooded slats often painted green, were also used at this time.

Slipcovers for furniture extended the protection of expensive upholstery. Loose coverings in striped linen or calico, gingham, and glazed chintz were kept on chairs to the extent that Lady Helen Hall wrote to the directors of the Assembly Rooms in Edinburgh requesting they "permit the covers of the sofas & benches . . . to be given out on the nights of the Dancing school balls . . . for nobody likes to sit upon dirty canvas with nails standing out, to tear their cloaths every time they move." Sheraton even mentions "covers for pier tables, made of stamped leather and glazed, lined with flannel to save the varnish of such table tops." During the mania for festoons, backs of chairs were modestly attired with a swag tacked to the back of the crest rail, as well as to the front of the seat rail.

Furniture

I think no room looks really comfortable, or even quite furnished without two tables—one to keep the wall . . . the other to stand here, there, and everywhere.

—Fanny Burney, diarist

Admitting comfort and convenience into the drawing room had radical repercussions for furniture. Of course, all sorts of furniture that encouraged lounging was in high demand, but the new concept that furniture was left in the middle of the room meant that items needed to be fully finished on all sides, as well as portable or pushable. Castors were attached to the bottom of anything that might be moved, which was almost everything.

The last vestiges of the cabriole leg and serpentine line were ironed out, and furniture took on a dignified rectilinear shape with the shield-back chair replaced by the square-back. The commode's lines smoothed out and morphed into a rectangular side cabinet, or chiffonier, surmounted with shelves for books. The beloved

ABOVE
A mirrored interior optimizes display on this Scottish ormolu-mounted amboyna cabinet, circa 1825, which stands just over five feet high.

LEFT
The Scottish display cabinet above displayed in situ circa 1880 at Coodham, Ayrshire, the home of Captain James Ogilvy-Fairley. It was originally en suite with a matching cabinet and pedestal cabinet underneath the large mirror.

Tables and chairs stand at ease in the middle of the Library-Drawing Room at Bromley Hill House, country house of Sir Charles Long, by John Chessell Buckley, 1816.

The klismos chair, with sabre legs and tablet-form back, was the quintessential Regency chair, as seen here on this black-japanned pair in a coolly elegant entrance hall by Cullman and Kravis.

oval of Adam was applied as shaped veneers to the doors of cabinets and secretaries and was evoked in the newly fashionable cylinder-front bureaus. Early Regency furniture was often made on a smaller, lighter scale than before, which befitted the need to move items around the room. Even the wall pieces, like secretaries and cabinets, were frequently reduced in height and depth to keep in proportion with the rest of the furnishings.

Castors were particularly useful as furniture became progressively more massive and ponderous at the end of the century, mimicking ancient bronze and marble furniture in mahogany and rosewood. Chairs, guided by "the pure taste of the antique reproduction of antique Greek forms of chairs," transformed. Sir Walter Scott observed:

> An ordinary chair in the most ordinary parlour has now something of an antique cast, something of Grecian massiveness, at once, and elegance in its form, that of twenty or

thirty years since was mounted on four tapering and tottering legs, resembling four tobacco pipes; the present supporters of our stools have a curule air, curve outwards behind and give a comfortable idea of stability to the weighty aristocrat or ponderous burgess who is about to occupy one of them.

The klismos form of chair, seen on the Hegeso stele, one of the most famous pieces of sculpture dating to 410 BC in Athens and on ancient Greek vases, soon attracted legions of devoted fans; it was described as "beyond comparison the coziest in which [one] ever sat down." The shift from the hoopskirt to the Empire chemise enabled sitters to enjoy its new sleek lines. It featured a horizontal tablet form and concave back support, on inward-curving, or sabre, legs. The klismos leg was so popular, it was used for tables as well.

Lounging was done on various permutations of the couch, also referred to as a daybed or chaise lounge. It was distinguished by a single-end support to rest

A Regency chaise longue provides respite and high glamour in this landing in a private residence.

FOLLOWING PAGES
This rosewood and brass-inlaid daybed, circa 1815, is related to the one in Thomas Hope's Egyptian Room.

This sumptuous rosewood sofa table, circa 1815, is beautifully fitted with ormolu mounts and finely inlaid with brass.

against, and in its earliest incarnation in antiquity, it was used for reclining while eating. Now associated with the female domain as all things intensely fashionable were, the couch was a must for the boudoir or dressing room, and often featured scroll-form ends recalling Apollo's lyre.

With furniture allowed to sit in the middle of the room permanently, the need for a table in front of the sofa was met. An elongated version of the pembroke, the new sofa table, was extremely versatile and used for sewing, taking tea, and reading. That England was the first to relax its furniture arrangements is perhaps why the sofa table was first seen in that country.

LEFT

A bold calamander center table anchors this grand room at Lord Mountbatten's Moyns Park.

TOP

This burr elm, marquetry, and parcel-gilt octagonal center table, circa 1820, is conceived in the Greek Revival manner of Thomas Hope.

ABOVE

A hinged compartment on the top of this octagonal "rent" table, circa 1775, was used to collect the rent from tenants and store documents relating to one's properties.

So beloved was the round table that it was brought into all rooms, where it stood dramatically in the center. Center tables were customized to serve any need, with leather tops for writing, drawers in the frieze for storage, a central lidded compartment on top as seen on rent tables, and even with a superstructure of rotating bookshelves.

The central pedestal or tripod support on center tables was used on tables of all sizes, including the conventional fold-over card tables. French-influenced spindly ring-turned legs resembling bamboo were used on the plethora of small tables praised by Fanny Burney. Tatham's monopodia, which appeared in Hope's and Smith's books and which were criticized for looking unfriendly and too monster-like, were applied to sideboards, center tables, and more. The dolphin and eagle, recalling those of William Kent, reappeared. The eagle, Napoleon's symbol, was immensely fashionable after the emperor's retreat from Russia in 1812. Classical lyre- and curule-form end supports were used extensively for smaller tables, including the new sofa table.

Dining tables at the end of the eighteenth century were no longer made of a series of tables that, when not in use, could be folded up and used as side tables. Now, they were raised on "pillars and claws" or central pedestal supports which

A mahogany dining table, circa 1805, looks perfectly matched with a set of twelve earlier "Chippendale" chairs. Thomas Sheraton stressed that in the dining room "the furniture, without exception, is of mahogany, as being the most suitable for such apartments."

The mechanism to extend this circular mahogany dining table, circa 1835, by Johnstone, Jupe and Co. was patented by Robert Jupe in March 1835. Only Johnstone and Jupe, who were in business until 1840, were able to manufacture this table until the patent ran out decades later, making this table a rarity.

This oval mahogany breakfast table, circa 1810, was the latest in table design and was made even more fashionable with an inlaid Greek-key border.

Commanding monopodia support a
Regency sideboard in this dining room.

ABOVE
The massive eagle supports on this
side table, from a pair, circa 1825, is
evocative of the work of William Kent
and his followers.

Swans, emblems of Venus, enrich the pedestal supports of a pair of fold-over games tables, which double beautifully as side tables in this sophisticated yet cozy sitting room by David Kleinberg. The swan motif was first used by Percier and Fontaine in the decoration of furniture for the palace of Saint Cloud, the main headquarters of Napoleon.

ended in four downswept (or sabre) legs, instead of legs set at the corners. This model could be as long as desired—more pedestal sections could be added by hinging them together with metal clips—with leaves in between. The dining parlor at Carlton House illustrated by Sheraton shows this type of table.

Round tables for dining were also highly desirable for "avoiding distinction of guests." English writer and poet laureate Robert Southey observed:

> Our breakfast table [important for the new breakfast rooms] is oval, large enough for eight or nine persons, yet supported upon one claw in the centre. This is the newest fashion, and fashions change so often in these things, as well as in every thing else, that it is easy to know how long it is since a house has been filled up, by the shape of the furniture.

Mirrors swelled to an enormous size and were often placed facing each other "to produce an effect of splendour." The upper plate was commonly treated with a reverse painted picture of a landscape or seascape or with *verre églomisé* decoration applied in gold leaf to the underside of the glass which was then engraved. The

FACING PAGE
Specimen marble tops were collected enthusiastically on the Grand Tour and brought back to England where appropriately impressive stands were made to support them, as here on this diminutive table in a sitting room by Connie Beale.

ABOVE
Quartetto tables, a set of four in graduated sizes, were the ultimate in portability and, when not in use, were compactly nested into each other.

RIGHT
Spindle-end supports, as on this plum-pudding library table attributed to Gillows (from a pair), were derived from French designs.

round convex mirror was brought over from France in 1795 and was applauded for its virtues of concentrating light and taking off "the coarseness of objects by contrasting them." Mirror plates were also inserted under side tables, held in place by the newly ubiquitous plinth base.

The tradesman Thomas Martin noted: "it is the fashion of the present day, to resort to a number of contrivances for making one piece of furniture serve many purposes," and Sheraton included several designs for harlequin furniture. Games tables appeared that included backgammon and chess boards, and metamorphic furniture, such as the chair that folded over into library steps, was all the rage. The firm of Gillows, which was established in Lancaster in the early eighteenth century and opened a London shop on Oxford Road in 1769, was experimental with their furniture design. They patented their extending Imperial Dining Table in 1800 and developed the distinctive campaign style davenport desk, as well as the first revolving bookcases.

Life was made more convenient by the advent of innumerable types of specialty furniture. The English love of after-dinner drinking necessitated the dumbwaiter—or serving trolley. The étagère, or whatnot, appeared at the end of the century as an open-shelved stand where a variety of objects could be displayed—definitely newly desirable in the cluttered and varied Regency interior. Portfolio and music stands were in demand as the pianoforte was "in almost every drawing room, from that of the humble tradesman, to that of the palace" by 1833. The cult of the library meant bookcases in all sizes and shapes were devised, including ones that could stand in the

Curule-end supports on this satinwood sofa table make a fashionably classical statement.

FACING PAGE
Beautifully carved giltwood dolphins support a marble slab on this formal center table, circa 1815.

The new model of a pillar and claw table allowed for a table to be as long as desired with the addition of another pedestal section. This is a three-pedestal example, circa 1810, which could be further extended with a leaf between each section.

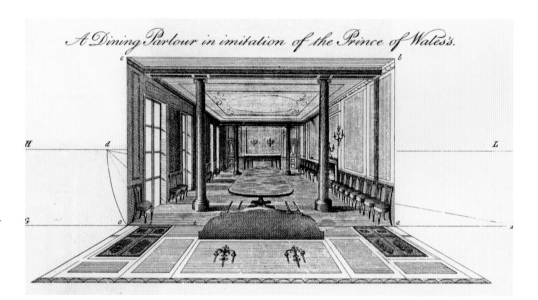

RIGHT

Thomas Sheraton's design of a dining parlour "gives a general idea of the Prince of Wales's in Carlton House . . . In the middle are placed a large range of dining tables, standing on pillars with four claws each, which is now the fashionable way of making these tables."

FACING PAGE

A lavishly ormolu-mounted library table becomes sculpture in this dramatic, pared down arrangement by David Kleinberg for Parish Hadley.

middle of the floor. Grilles, or "lacquered wirework fillings for bookcase doors," were now popular and were an option to glazing bars. New varieties of freestanding desks were developed, such as the elegant Carlton House model, so-called by Sheraton after one he saw at the Prince of Wales's London house.

The most opulent furniture was made from imported exotic woods, testament to Britain's vast overseas empire. Golden satinwood, used as the predominant timber until 1800, was joined by the deep purplish rosewood from Brazil, calamander from Ceylon, and amboyna from the Moluccas. The rarest of all, zebrawood, was so scarce that by 1820 "no more of it was to be had for love or money." Rosewood, a close-grained hard wood used for veneering, was held "in the highest esteem as a fancy wood," and used liberally for fashionable furniture. Calamander from the ebony family was also very fashionable with its contrasting stripes of black and yellow and its hardy, glossy sheen and was called "by far the most beautiful of the fancy woods." The high shine of French polish, introduced in Britain after the Napoleonic Wars in 1814, brought the surface of these exotic hard woods even closer to resembling marble, and its reflective gleam was decoration in itself.

War-time belt-tightening made inlaid furniture prohibitively expensive. Sheraton explained it as "a very expensive mode of decorating furniture used in the cabinet-making of twenty or thirty years back." Instead, employing contrasting

FACING PAGE
The large brass-inlaid pedestal desk in the hall at Hackwood Park was made en suite with the reading table at left by Gillows.

LEFT
This brass-inlaid reading table made for the second Baron Bolton at Hackwood Park by Gillows, circa 1810, has ratcheted side supports that can adjust the height of the top to accommodate reading.

ABOVE LEFT
This rosewood étagère, often called a whatnot, circa 1805, was refined with the addition of a ratcheted top with brass gallery.

ABOVE RIGHT
The doors of this satinwood collector's cabinet, circa 1815, enclose rows of small drawers that serve as a repository for an array of curiosities.

Fox-Nahem Designs create a sleek modern dining room with antiques by incorporating a minimum of furnishings and selecting bold silhouettes. A serving trolley stands by with a decanter and glasses.

A mahogany canterbury, circa 1815, which was stocked with music for the ubiquitous piano forte, is appropriately decorated with a lyre.

While the piano forte is no longer a prerequisite of the fashionable home, this rosewood canterbury, formerly used as a music stand, is ready to stow magazines and newspapers in this charming room by Brian J. McCarthy and Associates.

This satinwood and mahogany secretaire bookcase, circa 1805, was part of a suite of dressing and secretaire cabinets that incorporated clocks and automatic organs and were exhibited at the Thomas Weeks' Museum of Mechanical Curiosities in the Haymarket. Each secretaire was inset with a clock signed "Weeks' Museum."

FACING PAGE BOTTOM
The Carlton House desk was particularly desirable as it was fully finished on all sides and stands gracefully in the center of a room. Thomas Sheraton described it as a "Lady's Drawing and Writing Table."

ABOVE LEFT
A giltwood mirror, circa 1810, inset with a charming verre églomisé *panel is hung over a diminutive rosewood side table with monopodium supports.*

ABOVE RIGHT
Fantastical beasts, such as an outstretched dragon with a forked tongue and a pair of hippocampi, stallions with fish tails, enrich this extraordinary giltwood and ebonized convex mirror, circa 1815.

FACING PAGE
Maxwell Residence, Long Island, New York, 1970s. Interior with sofa and mirror. Parish Hadley Archive, Cooper-Hewitt National Design Museum, Smithsonian Institution.

A border-glass mirror opens up this sitting room by Parish Hadley and brings the verdant outdoors and luminous light inside.

veneers was used to achieve dramatic affects. Bandings of kingwood, tulipwood, rosewood, and purpleheart were used on pale satinwood pieces.

Around 1810 inlaid brass into rosewood became more popular. The ornament was cut out of a thin sheet of brass and inlaid into the veneer. The designs tended to be simple and grew fussier further into the century. Brass beaded molding also replaced wood moldings—this was a simple way to add glamour to a piece as well as reinforce its edges.

Carving continued to wane, and by the early nineteenth century, there were only eleven master carvers in London. The decline of carving was paralleled by the rise of cast-metal mounts for furniture. Ormolu mounts, made of gilt metal, were the most expensive and dangerous. The prince employed a French émigré craftsman in Sloane Square to cast mounts for Carlton House in brass or bronze, which were then fire gilt with mercury and gold. Another cheaper and safer method, as practiced by the celebrated supplier Matthew Boulton, was to cover brass mounts in lacquer gilding.

After the restoration of the Bourbon monarchy in France in 1814, an interest in the Louis XIV style came back. Boulle work, with its inlaid marquetry arabesque panels in metal or wood, was popular enough for the French émigré cabinetmaker

FACING PAGE
The muted palette of this sitting room sets off the high glamour of an elaborately mounted rosewood side cabinet.

ABOVE AND LEFT
Magnificent gilt-metal mounts, as on this rosewood side cabinet, circa 1820, became fashionable as carved decoration declined.

This type of reading chair is sometimes called a "cock-fighting" chair. A gentleman straddles the splat and can adjust the reading stand's position by sliding it along the crest rail.

Louis Le Gaigneur to open his own Buhl Manufactory around 1815, supplying none other than the Prince Regent. The cabinetmaker George Bullock, located in Hanover Square, did Buhlwork in woods. A true nationalist, his inlaid decoration was based on native vegetation such as oak leaves and hops, not just classical motifs. He also had a preference for native woods such as oak and larch in addition to imported exotic ones. Bullock's solid furniture was approvingly considered "of true Grecian taste, sharp, bold and well relieved."

The ebony furniture of André-Charles Boulle made for Louis XIV promoted the fashion of black-painted furniture. Black was particularly favored for painted furniture in an antiquarian interior as it was associated with age. Old oak furniture was extremely dark or even blackened. Caned seats and backs on japanned and painted chairs were the rule and reinforced their informality. In general painted furniture was found suitable for furnishing bedrooms, villas, and cottages.

The striking black-and-white penwork furniture was made by professional specialists and genteel ladies alike. Tea caddies to sofa tables were treated to the decoration of contrasting black and white, which, due to the yellowing of its protective coating of shellac, has usually turned a rich golden amber color. Decoration culled from the latest printed sources of classical scenes, Gothic ruins, and chinoiserie, was most commonly applied with black paint to a white base (or the reverse), with India ink line engraving applied with a quill pen providing additional detailing.

This rosewood and "Boulle work" cabinet is typical of the workshop of the French émigré cabinetmaker Louis LeGaigneur, who produced furniture for the Prince Regent and other members of the nobility.

ABOVE
*A brass mount of Apollo and the
contra partie panels on this rosewood
cabinet attributed to John McClean
look back to the work of André-Charles
Boulle for Louis XIV.*

RIGHT
*George Bullock relished using materials
and decoration native to England, as
exercised on this oak side cabinet with
foliate decoration.*

FACING PAGE
*The shallow dimensions and storage
space of Regency side cabinets make this
item extremely useful in smaller spaces.
Its clean lines help it mix beautifully
with more modern elements, as with the
painting overhead here in this vignette
by Cullman and Kravis.*

RIGHT ABOVE & BELOW
The top of this exquisite penwork work table, circa 1815, is decorated with chinoiserie figures playing musical instruments.

FACING PAGE
The sides, interior, and frieze of this spectacular penwork cabinet, circa 1815, are all decorated with scenes from the Iliad, after Flaxman's celebrated illustrations to Homer's epic.

❧ ❧ ❧

The earth-shattering concept that interiors could be visually impressive and comfortable was just as revolutionary a notion at the time as were the concurrent advances in technology. The obsessive fascination the British held for the classical world swept them away as they time-traveled back to ancient Rome and Greece in their rosewood reproductions of couches and klismos chairs. Luckily for them, floor plans weren't depicted on their Etruscan vases, and they were free to give into the seductions of the natural world and indulge their inherent desires for comfort and convenience.

The Regency period capped off a century in which the applied arts were constantly refined and, guided by the Prince Regent's indefatigable patronage, ultimately brought to a superlative level. It also heralded the end of an era as the Industrial Revolution dawned, when machines soon took over the manufacturing of household goods, and the ever-prized qualities of novelty and innovation were pushed aside for the Victorian pastiche of styles.

The gilt-metal mounts strategically applied on this small Regency table catch the light, adding flashes of glitter to this dark paneled room by David Kleinberg Design Associates.

Matthew Boulton was famous for his lavishly ormolu-mounted Blue John tazzas, similar to the one here, circa 1810.

PICTORIAL HISTORY OF FURNITURE STYLES

CHAIRS

QUEEN ANNE WALNUT SIDE CHAIR
(FROM A PAIR), CIRCA 1705.
*A shaped vasiform backsplat makes chairs more
comfortable than ever, and the cabriole leg is
introduced.*

GEORGE II MAHOGANY ARMCHAIR,
CIRCA 1725.
*The backsplat shrinks and becomes more of a
"hoop" shape, mirroring the shape of the human
body. Simple classical ornament is carved, and the
stretcher is no longer necessary with the new use
of mahogany.*

GEORGE II WALNUT ARMCHAIR,
CIRCA 1750.
*A good example of the many variations
on the interlaced backsplat, as seen in
Thomas Chippendale's* Director.

GEORGE III PAINTED SHIELD–BACK OPEN
ARMCHAIR, CIRCA 1780.
*Flat decoration was the foundation of Robert
Adam's Neoclassicism and is used on this chair.
The shield back was popularized in the designs
of George Hepplewhite.*

REGENCY MAHOGANY KLISMOS CHAIR,
CIRCA 1795.
*An exceedingly popular form taken directly from
examples from antiquity; sabre legs and the tablet-
form backsplat became ubiquitous.*

GEORGE IV MAHOGANY ARMCHAIR,
CIRCA 1830.
*The late Regency's characteristic heaviness
is evident on this boldly carved armchair.*

WILLIAM AND MARY WALNUT AND OYSTER-VENEERED
CHEST OF DRAWERS, CIRCA 1690.
*The skilled application of walnut veneers with contrasting line inlays
bears testament to the increasing sophistication of England's furniture
makers and the period's taste for ornamentation.*

GEORGE I WALNUT BACHELOR'S CHEST,
CIRCA 1720.
*A taste for simplicity marks this plain chest of drawers with bookmatched
veneers. As dovetailing became more widespread, chests like this one were
increasingly available to the middle class.*

GEORGE III MAHOGANY COMMODE,
CIRCA 1760.
*The Rococo's serpentine line transforms the shape of this chest
of drawers, now called a commode after French examples.*

GEORGE III SATINWOOD AND INLAID COMMODE,
CIRCA 1775.
*The husk garlands and classical urns popularized by
Robert Adam are inlaid into this modified Rococo shape.*

REGENCY AMBOYNA AND EBONIZED CHIFFONIER,
CIRCA 1790.
*The severe form and engaged colonettes are characteristic of the early
Regency made popular by the Prince of Wales at Carlton House and
influenced heavily by the French Directoire style.*

GEORGE IV BRASS INLAID AND MOUNTED ROSEWOOD SIDE
CABINET, CIRCA 1830.
*A preference for dark exotic woods and a renewed taste for the Louis
XIV period's gilt-metal mounts and inlaid "Boulle" work are expressed
in this elaborate cabinet.*

SIDE TABLES

WILLIAM AND MARY WALNUT AND SEAWEED MARQUETRY
SIDE TABLE, CIRCA 1695.
*The Baroque's emphasis on pattern and movement are displayed
here on the spiral-turned legs (often referred to as "barley twist")
and the intricate arabesque inlay.*

GEORGE I WALNUT SIDE TABLE,
CIRCA 1720.
*This simple table, with clean lines and raised on the new cabriole
leg, found many admirers who prized its plainness and found
the Baroque distastefully ornate.*

GEORGE II MAHOGANY MARBLE-TOP SIDE TABLE,
CIRCA 1750. *Claw-and-ball feet replace pad feet, and a profusion
of ornament is carved into the hard-grained mahogany.*

GEORGE III SATINWOOD AND INLAID DEMI-LUNE SIDE TABLE,
CIRCA 1780.
*Satinwood and inlaid decoration are embraced during the Neoclassical
style, and the square, tapering leg reflects the period's preference for lighter,
more controlled shapes.*

REGENCY ROSEWOOD AND PARCEL GILT SIDE TABLE,
CIRCA 1795.
*Rich rosewood contrasting with gilt fluted legs creates a dramatic
and severe look derived from the French Directoire style and used
by Henry Holland for Carlton House.*

REGENCY MAHOGANY AND GILT METAL MOUNTED SIDE TABLE,
CIRCA 1815.
*The late Regency's archaeological approach to design is demonstrated
on the lion monopodia supports and the massive size relieved sparingly
with classical ornament.*

WILLIAM AND MARY WALNUT AND FLORAL MARQUETRY CUSHION MIRROR, CIRCA 1690. *The detachable, shaped cresting reflects the period's penchant for the arch, while its small size was determined by the prohibitive cost and the inability to make larger plates.*

QUEEN ANNE PIER MIRROR, CIRCA 1705. *An arched upper plate replaces the detachable cresting and adds height.*

GEORGE I GILT GESSO MIRROR, CIRCA 1720. *The rectilinear form and beginnings of a swan's neck pediment marks the transition from Baroque to Palladian.*

GEORGE II GILTWOOD MIRROR, CIRCA 1735. *The fully developed architectural pediment reflects the new Palladian style.*

GEORGE III GILTWOOD MIRROR,
CIRCA 1765.
*The exuberantly carved C-scrolls and
whimsical ornament, such as a Chinese
man incorporated into the cresting, is
characteristic of the English Rococo.*

GEORGE III GILTWOOD MIRROR,
CIRCA 1775.
*Adam's influence is evident in the oval
shape and Neoclassical ornament.*

GILTWOOD CONVEX MIRROR SURMOUNTED
BY AN EAGLE, CIRCA 1805.
*Newly brought over from France, this convex mirror
was of the latest fashion.*

GEORGE IV GILTWOOD OVERMANTEL MIRROR,
CIRCA 1825.
*The archaeological heaviness of the late Regency is evidenced
in this mirror's bold carving and heavy proportions.*

BUREAU BOOKCASES

WILLIAM AND MARY FLORAL MARQUETRY
CABINET-ON-STAND, CIRCA 1695.
*Cabinets were rare and therefore emblems of status,
executed in as high style as its owner could afford.*

QUEEN ANNE WALNUT DOUBLE-DOME BUREAU CABINET,
CIRCA 1710.
*The cabinet is placed on a desk and chest of drawers. Daniel Marot's
use of the arch translates into the double-dome pediment.*

GEORGE I SCARLET AND GILT JAPANNED BUREAU CABINET,
CIRCA 1725.
*An architectural broken-arch pediment is applied to this
Palladian bureau cabinet.*

GEORGE II MAHOGANY BUREAU BOOKCASE,
CIRCA 1750. *In this example, the desk and chest become one
piece.*

GEORGE III SATINWOOD SECRETAIRE BOOKCASE WITH
ROSEWOOD CROSSBANDING, CIRCA 1780.
The secretaire drawer replaces the slant front, and golden satinwood,
which harmonizes with the Adam interior, is preferred.

REGENCY ROSEWOOD AND SATINWOOD SECRETAIRE BOOKCASE
WITH PAINTED DECORATION, CIRCA 1790.
Smaller proportions, cubic proportions, and inlaid oval panels are all
early Regency characteristics.

GEORGE IV MAHOGANY SECRETAIRE BOOKCASE,
CIRCA 1825. *The triangular pediment, taken from the roofs of ancient*
Greek houses according to Thomas Hope, was used extensively in the
late Regency.

BIBLIOGRAPHY

Period Sources

Ackermann, Rudolph. *The Repository of Arts, Literature, Commerce, Manufactures, Fashions and Politics.* London: published in volume form from 1809 to 1828.

Adam, Robert and James. *Works in Architecture.* 2 vols. London: n.p., 1773.

Campbell, Colen. *Vitruvius Britannicus, or the British Architect.* London: n.p., 1725.

Chippendale, Thomas. *The Gentleman and Cabinet-Maker's Director.* London: n.p., 1754, 1755, and 1762.

The Collection of Rare Prints & Illustrated Works, Removed from Strawberry Hill for Sale in London. London: Smith & Robins, 1842.

Daniell, Thomas and William. *Oriental Scenery.* London: n.p., 1808.

Flaxman, John. *The Odyssey of Homer.* London: Longman, Hurst, Rees & Orme, 1805.

Gibbs, James. *A Book of Architecture, Containing Designs of Buildings and Ornaments.* London: n.p., 1728.

d'Hancarville, Pierre-François Hugues. *Antiquités Etrusques, Grecques et Romaines. Tirées du Cabinet de M. Hamilton.* 1767.

Hepplewhite, George. *The Cabinet-Maker and Upholsterer's Guide.* London: n.p., 1788.

Hope, Thomas. *Household Furniture and Interior Decoration.* London: T. Bensley, 1804.

Ince, William, and John Mayhew. *Universal System of Household Furniture.* London: n.p., 1762.

Jones, William. *The Gentlemen's or Builders Companion.* London: n.p., 1739.

Kent, William, ed. *The Designs of Inigo Jones.* London, 1727.

Langley, Batty. *The City and Country Builder's and Workman's Treasury of Designs.* London: n.p., 1740.

Lock, Matthias. *A New Drawing Book of Ornaments, Shields, Compartments, Masks.* London: n.p., 1740.

Loudon, John Claudius. *An Encyclopedia of Cottage, Farm, and Villa Architecture and Furniture.* London: n.p., 1835.

Marot, Daniel. *Oeuvres du Sr. D. Marot, Architecte de Guilliuame III, Roy de la Grande Bretagne.* Amsterdam: n.p., 1712.

——. *Das ornamentwerk des Daniel Marot in 264 lichtdrucken nachgebildet.* Berlin: E. Wasmuth, 1892.

Nash, John. *Views of the Royal Pavilion.* 1826.

Palladio, Andrea. *Andrea Palladio's Five Orders of Architecture.* Revised by Colen Campbell. London: S. Harding, 1729.

Percier, Charles, and Pierre Francois Leonard Fontaine. *Recueil de décorations intérieures, comprenant tout ce qui a Rapport a l'Ameublement.* Paris: A. Guérinet, 1812.

Piranesi, Giovanni Battista. *Vasi, Candelabri, Cippi, Sarcofagi.* 2 vols. Rome: n.p., 1778.

Pyne, W. H. *The History of the Royal Residences of Windsor Castle, St. James's Palace, Carlton House, and Frogmore.* London: n.p., 1819.

Repton, Humphry. *Fragments on the Theory and Practice of Landscape Gardening.* London: n.p., 1816.

Sheraton, Thomas. *The Cabinet Dictionary.* Vols. I and II. 1803; reissued New York: Praeger, 1970.

———. *The Cabinet-Maker and Upholsterer's Drawing-Book*. London: T. Bensley, 1802.

Smith, George. *A Collection of Designs for Household Furniture and Interior Decoration*. London: n.p., 1808.

Stalker, John, and George Parker. *A Treatise of Japanning and Varnishing*. London: n.p., 1688.

Stuart, James, and Nicholas Revett. *Antiquities of Athens*. London: n.p., 1762.

Tatham, C. H. *Etchings of Ancient Ornamental Architecture drawn from the Originals in Rome and Other Parts of Italy during the years 1794, 1795, and 1796*. London: n.p., 1799, 1800.

Vardy, John. *Some Designs of Mr. Inigo Jones and of Mr. William Kent*. London: n.p., 1744.

Winckelmann, Johann Joachim. *Reflections on the Imitation of Greek Works in Painting and Sculpture*. 1755.

Wood, Robert. *The Ruins of Palmyra*. London: n.p., 1753.

Diaries, Letters, and Memoirs

Bessborough, Henrietta Frances Spencer Ponsonby, Countess of. *Lady Bessborough and Her Family Circle*. Edited by the Earl of Bessborough, G.C.M.G. in collaboration with A. Aspinall. London: J. Murray, 1940.

Burney, Fanny. *The Early Journals and Letters of Fanny Burney*. Edited by Lars E. Troide. Oxford: Clarendon Press, 1988.

Defoe, Daniel. *A Tour thro' the Whole Island of Great Britain . . . by a Gentleman*. 3 vols. London: G. Strahan, 1724–27.

Edgeworth, Maria. *Letters from England 1813–1844*. Edited by Christina Colvin. Oxford: Clarendon Press, 1971.

Evelyn, John. *The Diary of Sir John Evelyn*. Edited by William Bray. New York: M. W. Dunne, 1901.

———. *Silva; or, A discourse of Forest-trees, and the Propagation of Timber in His Majesty's Dominions*. London: H. Colburn, 1825.

Evelyn, Mary. *Mundus muliebris*. London: n.p., 1690.

Fiennes, Celia. *The Journeys of Celia Fiennes*. Edited by Christopher Morris. London: Cresset Press, 1949.

Minto, Countess of. *Life and letters of Sir Gilbert Elliot, First Earl of Minto, from 1751 to 1806*. London: Longmans, Green and Co., 1874.

Montagu, Elizabeth. *The Letters of Mrs. Elizabeth Montagu*. Boston: Wells and Lilly, 1825.

Shaftesbury, Anthony Ashley Cooper. *Characteristicks of Men, Manners, Opinions, Times*. London: n.p., 1714.

Southey, Robert. *Letters from England: by Don Manuel Espriella*. New York: David Longworth, 1808.

Walpole, Horace. *Letters of Horace Walpole*. Edited by W.S. Lewis. London: Folio Society, 1951.

Contemporary Sources

Baarsen, Renier, Gervase Jackson-Stops, Phillip Johnston, and Elaine Dee. *Courts and Colonies: the William and Mary Style in Holland, England, and America*. New York: Cooper-Hewitt National Design Museum, 1988.

Beard, Geoffrey. *The National Trust Book of the English House Interior*. London: Penguin, 1991.

Beard, Geoffrey. *Upholsterers and Interior Furnishing in England: 1530–1840*. New Haven: Yale University Press, 1997.

Boynton, Lindsay, ed. *Gillow Furniture Designs: 1760–1800*. Royston, Hertfordshire: Bloomfield Press, 1995.

Bowett, Adam. *English Furniture: 1660–1714 from Charles II to Queen Anne*. Woodbridge, England: Antique Collectors' Club, 2002.

Collard, Frances. *Regency Furniture*. Woodbridge, Suffolk: Antique Collector's Club, 1987.

Cornforth, John. *Early Georgian Interiors*. New Haven: Yale University Press, 2004.

Friedman, Joseph. *Spencer House: Chronicle of a Great London Mansion*. London: Zwemmer, 1993.

George Bullock Cabinet Maker. Exhibition catalogue. H. Blairman and Sons: John Murray, 1988.

Gilbert, Christopher. *The Life and Work of Thomas Chippendale*. 2 vols. New York: Macmillan, 1978.

Girouard, Mark. *Life in the English Country House: a Social and Architectural History*. New Haven: Yale University Press, 1978.

Harris, Eileen. *The Furniture of Robert Adam*. London: A. Tiranti, 1963.

———. *The Genius of Robert Adam: His Interiors*. New Haven: Yale University Press, 2001.

Hayward, Helena, and Pat Kirkham. *William and John Linnell, Eighteenth-Century London Furniture Makers*. 2 vols. New York: Rizzoli, 1980.

Jackson-Stops, Gervase, ed. *Treasure Houses of Britain: Five Hundred Years of Private Patronage and Art Collecting*. New Haven: Yale University Press, 1985.

Jaffer, Amin. *Furniture from British India and Ceylon*. Salem, Mass.: Peabody Essex Museum in association with V&A Publications, 2001.

Jourdain, Margaret. *Chinese Export Art in the Eighteenth Century*. London: Country Life, 1950.

Jourdain, Margaret, and F. Rose. *English Furniture: the Georgian Period (1750–1830)*. London: Batsford, 1953.

Morley, John. *History of Furniture*. Boston: Little, Brown and Company, 1999.

Murdoch, Tessa. "Jean, René and Thomas Pelletier, Huguenot family of carvers and gilders in England, 1682–1726, Part I." *The Burlington Magazine* (November 1997): 732–42.

Riccardi-Cubitt, Monique. *The Art of the Cabinet*. London: Thames and Hudson, 1992.

Saumarez Smith, Charles. *Eighteenth-century Decoration: Design and the Domestic Interior in England*. London: Weidenfeld and Nicolson, 1993.

Symonds, R. W. *English Furniture from Charles II to George II*. London: The Connoisseur, 1929.

Thornton, Peter. *Authentic Décor—The Domestic Interior, 1620–1920*. New York: Viking, 1984.

Ward-Jackson, Peter. *English Furniture Designs of the Eighteenth Century*. London: Victoria and Albert Museum, 1958.

Watkin, David. *The Royal Interiors of Regency England*. London: Vendome Press, 1984.

Wilson, Michael I. *William Kent: Architect, Designer, Painter, Gardener, 1685–1748*. Boston: Routledge and Kegan Paul, 1984.

INDEX

Note: Page numbers in *italics* indicate both illustrations and captions.

PHOTO CREDITS

top: *t*
bottom: *b*
left: *l*
right: *r*

Bridgeman Art Library: 105 © The Trustees of the Weston Park Foundation, UK; 143 The Stapleton Collection, UK; 144 Victoria and Albert Museum, London; 147 © Townley Hall Art Gallery and Museum, Burnley, Lancashire, UK; 149 Private collection, The Stapleton Collection, UK; 176 Private collection; 207 © Apsley House, The Wellington Museum, London, UK; 208*b* © Louvre, Paris, France/Giraudon; 214–15 Royal Pavilion, Brighton, East Sussex, UK; 218 Private collection, The Stapleton Collection, UK; 222 Private collection/The Stapleton Collection, UK; 223 Private collection; 226 © Private Collection/The Stapleton Collection, UK; 228 The Stapleton Collection, UK; 230–31, 236–37 © Guildhall Library, City of London

© The Trustees of the British Museum: 151, 168*l*

Brunschwig & Fils/Room designed by Mario Buatta for the 1987 Kips Bay Show House, featuring Brunschwig & Fils Campanula Glazed Chintz: 7.

Charlotte Moss: 48, 224, 275

Christie's Images Ltd.: 186*l* © 1999; 221, 246 © 1993

Condé Nast Publications, Inc. Reprinted by permission. All Rights Reserved.
- John Hall/*Architectural Digest*, copyright © 2005: 8, 69, 73, 83, 95
- Durston Saylor/*Architectural Digest*, copyright © 2000: 204–5
- Billy Cunningham/*Architectural Digest*, copyright © 2000: 56
- Simon Upton/*House & Garden*, copyright © 2003: 59, 121, 245
- Michel Arnaud/*House & Garden*, copyright © 1998: 94

Connie Beale, Inc.: 256

Cooper-Hewitt, National Design Museum, Smithsonian Institution:
- Bequest of Marian Hague, 1971-71-5, photo by Matt Flynn: 13
- Museum purchase from General Acquisitions Endowment Fund, 1988-4-48, photo by Ken Pelka: 21
- Museum purchase from General Acquisitions Endowment Fund, 1988-4-57, photo by Scott Hyde: 35
- Purchased for the Museum by the Advisory Council, 1921-6-168, photo by Scott Hyde: 90
- Parish Hadley Archive, photo by Robert Ames Cook: 271

Country Life Picture Library: 47 (Tim Imrie), 66, 98 (Tim Imrie), 100–101 (Tim Imrie), 126, 158 (Juliam Nieman), 195 (Peter Aprahamian)

Cullman and Kravis: 130, 178, 239–40, 278

David Kleinberg Design Associates: 254, 283

Debra Blair Design Associates: 24

Dennis Krukowski Photography: 125, 167, 208, 261

Dennis Rolland Interior Design: 29, 169, 180

Courtesy of Drayton House: 17

© English Heritage Photographic Library: frontispiece, 50–51, 163

Courtesy of Fairfax House, York, England: 55

© Fritz von der Schulenberg/ The Interior Archive: 20, 36, 264

Hyde Park Antiques, Ltd./photography by Robert Lorenzson: 9, 22, 23, 25, 27, 31, 32, 33, 34, 37, 38, 40, 41, 42, 43*tr* and *b*, 44, 57, 58, 60, 61*b*, 63, 64*r*, 65, 67, 68, 70–71, 72, 76, 77, 78, 79*b*, 80, 82*t*, 85, 86, 87, 91, 102, 107, 109, 112*r*, 114,115, 116, 117, 118*t*, 120, 122, 124, 127, 129, 131, 132, 134–35, 136, 137, 138–39, 140, 141, 155, 164–65, 166, 168*r*, 170, 172, 173, 174, 175, 176*bl*, 177, 179, 181, 182, 183t, 184, 185, 187, 188, 189, 191, 192, 193, 194, 197, 198–99, 200, 201, 202, 213, 216*t*, 219, 227, 234, 235*r*, 240, 241, 242–43, 244, 247, 248, 249, 250, 251, 252, 253, 257, 258, 259, 260*t*, 262, 263, 265, 267, 268, 269, 270, 272, 273, 274, 276–77, 279, 280, 281, 282, 283*b*, 284–93.
Photography by William Marshall: 30, 82*b*, 113, 128*b*

National Gallery of Ireland: 154

© National Trust Photo Library:
- Bill Batten: 11, 145, 150
- Andreas von Einsiedel: 92–93, 96–97, 153
- John Hammond: 160
- James Mortimer: 232–33

The New York Public Library, Astor, Lenox and Tilden Foundations/Art & Architecture Collection, Miriam and Ira D. Wallach Division of Art, Prints and Photographs: 16, 28, 133, 217; Picture Collection, The Branch Libraries: 186*r*

The New York Times/Keith Meyers: 6

© Philadelphia Museum of Art, The John Howard McFadden Collection, 1928: 54

Phillip Ennis Photography: 74–75, 229

Pieter Estersohn: 266

Ralph Harvard Inc.: 110–11, 119

© Royal Academy of Arts, London: 156–57

Sam Gray Photography: 203

© Spencer House/Photo by Mark Fiennes, www.spencerhouse.co.uk: 148

Toledo Museum of Art: 161

V&A Images/Anonymous Loan to Victoria and Albert Museum: 81

Victoria and Albert Museum: 15, 43*l*, 49, 64*l*, 89, 162

Courtesy of the Viscount De L'Isle: 18–19

William Rush Jenkins: 39, 45, 62

Courtesy of the Earl of Pembroke and Montgomery and the Trustees of the Wilton House Trust: 53